The Fullness of Christ

BOOKS BY STUART BRISCOE . . .

Getting Into God

Living Dangerously

*Where Was the Church
    When the Youth Exploded?*

The Fullness of Christ

D. Stuart Briscoe

Introduction by
MAJOR W. IAN THOMAS

ZONDERVAN
PUBLISHING HOUSE

OF THE ZONDERVAN CORPORATION | GRAND RAPIDS, MICHIGAN 49506

Library of Congress Catalog Card No. 64-7846

Sixteenth printing 1977
ISBN 0-310-21712-1

NOTE: Many of the Scripture quotations in
this book are taken from *The Amplified New
Testament* and used by permission.

Printed in the United States of America

Contents

Introduction

Introduction

Secretary and Treasurer of the Capernwray Missionary Fellowship of Torchbearers of which it is my privilege to be the Founder and General Director, Stuart Briscoe is more fully occupied by far in evangelistic and convention ministry than he is in pushing the proverbial pen!

This public ministry has taken Stuart Briscoe beyond the boundaries of the British Isles into many countries of Western Europe, and from coast to coast on the Continent of North America, and if his desk in consequence is more often graced by his absence than by his presence — I am delighted indeed that he has taken this opportunity to minister in a wider way, through the printed pages of this book, to the hearts of so many who "hunger and thirst after righteousness," but who have never yet discovered that the Lord Jesus Christ Himself is "the Prelude, Pattern, Province and the Power of all Christian experience."

To discover that Christianity is *all of Him* in *all of you*" is to discover the heart of the Gospel, and the very dynamic of our faith; there is nothing more calculated than this to turn big babies into mature men!

Throughout the many years that I have known him, and more especially as it has been my joy increasingly to labor with him, I have come to regard both Stuart Briscoe and his devoted wife, together with their lovely little family, with deep affection, and I believe that God the Holy Spirit will bless the lively message of this book to your heart — for here is the

Truth, refreshing and clear, and expressed with all the natural warmth and excitement of one who has made the discovery for himself and feels compelled to pass it on; it is the reality of discovering *who* Christ is, and *where* Christ is, and to crown it all in the words of the Author, the thrilling reality of "*why* He is, *who* He is, *where* He is!" That is to say — "all of Him" being all that He is, and in "all of you" in all that you are!

"CHRIST IN YOU, the hope of glory" (Colossians 1:27).

W. IAN THOMAS

1

Mature Men

"THE CHILD IS FATHER OF THE MAN," SAID WORDSWORTH.
His statement expressed a basic principle of life which
we all understand. Babies have a habit of growing up
into adults. No one is surprised when little junior pro-
gresses from a recumbent posture to a furious crawl.
He doesn't stop there, but soon he develops a tottering
walk which in turn gives way to a manly gait, and in
all probability he will soon make breath-taking sprints
on the football field. He is maturing and growing up,
and this is perfectly natural.

In Luke 2:52 we read that "Jesus increased in wisdom and stature and in favour with God and man."
You will notice that His development was on four
planes. He increased in wisdom — *intellectually;* in stature — *physically;* in favor with God — *spiritually;* and
in favor with man — *socially.* Jesus, the boy-child of
Bethlehem, grew up to be the Man of Nazareth, and in
the process of growing and maturing, He outlined the
four planes of normal development. It is not the purpose of this book to investigate the *intellectual* and
physical development of "homo sapiens" but primarily
to discover what the Bible teaches about *spiritual*
growth and its repercussions upon *social* behavior.

It is quite obvious that the prerequisite to growth
is life, and spiritual growth is no exception to this rule.
Many people seem to have the mistaken impression

9

that spiritual maturity can be attained without spiritual life. Nicodemus, the pious ruler-teacher of Jerusalem in the first century, was startled out of his religious rut by the outspoken Lord when He said, "You must be born again." Nicodemus was physically mature, of outstanding intellectual ability and of the highest social standing, but his attempts at spiritual maturity were bound to fail because he was lacking in the one prerequisite — spiritual life!

Jesus also accused the Jews in John chapter 6 of having no life in them. Obviously, He was not referring to physical life, intellectual ability or social standing, but to a spiritual deadness which was painfully obvious in their daily lives, and which was underlined by their lack of spiritual understanding and perception in their dealings with Christ. It was so clear to the Lord Jesus — before spiritual maturity must come spiritual life, and before spiritual life must come spiritual birth!

To put it another way: before man can *increase* in favor with God, he must be *in* favor with God, and before he can be in favor, a revolution must take place to rectify his natural status which is *out of* favor with God. The Bible has much to say on the subject of man's natural status. According to Scripture, men are "alienated from the life of God" (Ephesians 4:18), "dead in trespasses and sins" (Ephesians 2:1), "children of God's wrath and heirs of his indignation" (Ephesians 2:3, Amplified New Testament), "estranged and alienated from Him and of hostile attitude of mind in wicked activities" (Colossians 1:21, Amplified New Testament). Therefore, man's great spiritual need is to be restored to contact and favor with his Maker, and then to experience a new quality of life which will possess all that he is, and reproduce through him the quality of life capable of pleasing the One who made him. That this is no minor problem is obvious — in fact, the problem is so immense that it is completely outside the capabilities of the most ingenious and gifted man either to reconcile himself to God, or to impart to himself new life.

"Who can forgive sins but God only?" (Mark 2:7), reasoned the scribes. How right they were! Sin is an attitude of heart, common to man, which repudiates God's right to possess what He made, control what He designed, and fulfill what He planned. Sin is a cold-blooded rebellion in which rebel man takes the law into his own hands, and overthrows the rule of the Sovereign God. Sin is always primarily anti-God, even though it may, and probably will have secondary repercussions on the society of which the sinner is a member. When man understands that sin opposes God, he should have no difficulty in recognizing that forgiveness of sin can only come from God. It would be ludicrous to suggest that a man, having sinned against God, could then have it within his power to forgive his own sin. If one man desires to punch another man on the nose, only the man with the broken nose can forgive his assailant! It would be ridiculous to suggest that the attacker could look at his battered opponent and say, "Don't worry, old fellow, I forgive me!" However, many men today appear to have the impression that they are quite capable of forgiving their own sin, and saying in effect to God, "Please don't worry — I am quite capable of forgiving me!" No — quite logically we must arrive at the conclusion at which the scribes arrived — "Who can forgive sins but God only?"

"Can a man enter his mother's womb again and be born?" (John 3:4), queried Nicodemus. Of course he cannot. Man is as incapable of organizing his spiritual birth as he was of dictating the terms of his physi-

cal birth. Man died to God as a direct result of his
sin, and quite obviously he has experienced a state of
spiritual deadness ever since. The Bible teaches that
man is God's creature living in God's world, made by
God, for God, to live unto God. If man has died to
God and lost contact with God, then there is only one
thing wrong — man is God-less. If God is excluded
from the Bible definition of man given above, what is
left? Man is *a* creature, living in *a* world, made *some-
how* for *something*, to live *somewhere!* What a nebulous, pointless existence this is, and yet this is the mean-
ingless principle upon which countless lives are being
lived today. A life lived on such a basis is a life which
demonstrates the awfulness of having been "alienated
from the life of God."

Can man rectify this position? If man got into this
condition as a result of God withdrawing His life
(spiritual death) from man, is it reasonable to suppose
that man can restore what God removed? Obviously
the answer is "no." Therefore, it will be seen that if
man's sin is to be forgiven and new life is to be imparted to him, God must take the initiative, because
man, for all his wisdom, is incapable of forgiving his
own sin or of reimparting divine life to himself. The
question that automatically comes to mind is this: Is
God willing and able to do for man what man cannot
do for himself?

The Scriptures proclaim loud and clear that God
is both able and willing to take the initiative — in fact,
that He has already done so! "If, when we were enemies, we were reconciled to God by the death of his
Son, much more being reconciled we shall be saved
by his life" (Romans 5:10). This is the answer. God,
through the death of His Son makes reconciliation,
restoration, and forgiveness of sin possible. Those

"*out of* favour" because of their rebellion, and enmity can be "*in* favour," but on one ground only. If God must do the forgiving and God must take the initiative, God must be allowed to dictate terms, and He says the only basis of forgiveness is "the death of his Son."

The perennial question of man is: Why is the death of His Son necessary? Couldn't God just forgive and forget? No — it is not so easy. God is a merciful, gracious, loving God as we can see in the gracious and loving gift of His Son to die on the cross, but He is also a righteous, just and holy God. This means that He can always be relied upon to do the right thing. Man expects God to *be* just, righteous and holy, and therefore logically he must expect God to *do* that which is just, righteous and holy, and that includes His dealings with sin.

Because He is *holy*, He *hates* sin; because He is *righteous*, He *rejects* sin and because He is *just*, He can be relied upon to *judge* sin. Therefore, we see that before God could forgive sin, He had to judge sin, either individually in the person of the sinner, or collectively in the person of a substitute. "God commendeth his love toward us, in that, while we were yet sinners, Christ died for us" (Romans 5:8).

The Sinless Substitute, Jesus Christ, died for my sin and yours, took the judgment against my sin and yours, and as a result God, having judged my sin, and yours in the Person of Christ, is now in a position to forgive our sin, and is ready for any sinner to meet with Him and be reconciled to Him — to have His status of "out-of-favour" completely changed to "in-favour" with God. Now the onus is upon each individual to respond to, or reject God's command, and invitation, "Be *ye* reconciled to God." Reconciliation can only take place when in repentance and faith, an individual thanks Christ for dying for him, and gladly abandons his life to the One who abandoned His life for him.

> Love so amazing, so divine,
> Demands my soul, my life, my all.

This answers half the problem, but it does not explain how a man can be born again or receive new life. Let us return to Romans 5:10 — ". . . much more being reconciled, we shall be saved by his life." Christ died that man might be reconciled, but rose again, and lives that man might be revitalized. He lives, so that by His Spirit He might come to live in a man's innermost being, to impart His life, and to make that man a "partaker of the divine nature" (II Peter 1:4). This revitalization or regeneration can only be experienced when a man recognizes his need of Christ, decides he wants Christ, and invites Christ to step into his life. Jesus Christ said, "Behold, I stand at the door and knock. If any man hear my voice and open the door, *I will* come in . . ." (Revelation 3:20). Scripture says, "He that hath the Son hath life; and he that hath not the Son of God, hath not life" (I John 5:12).

> Into my heart, into my heart,
> Come into my heart, Lord Jesus;
> Come in today,
> Come in to stay,
> Come into my heart, Lord Jesus.

So says the children's chorus, and these simple words can echo the heart-felt sentiments of any man who really means business, and on the basis of God's promises, new birth will be the inevitable consequence. "And as Moses lifted up the serpent in the wilderness, even so must the Son of man be lifted up: That whosoever believeth in him should not perish, but have eternal life. For God so loved the world, that he gave his only begotten Son, that whosoever believeth in him should not perish, but have everlasting life" (John 3:14-16).

Therefore, we see that when a man, recognizing his need of Christ, in sincere repentance and in child-like faith invites Christ to invade his life, two things take place:

(1) he is reconciled to God;

(2) he is born again of the Spirit of God.

This man becomes a Christian when he receives Christ. John 1:11, 12, in the Amplified New Testament, says, "He came to that which belonged to Him, to His own (domain, creation, things, world), and they who were His own did not receive Him and did not welcome Him. But to as many as did receive and welcome Him, He gave the authority (power, privilege, right) to become the children of God, that is, to those who believe in — adhere to, trust in and rely on — His name."

It is a serious mistake to think that God is only interested in forgiving sins and in saving souls from death. God is concerned that the man who has been forgiven, cleansed, reconciled and born again should now mature in his spiritual experience. As we have already seen in John 1:11, 12, when a person receives Christ, God regards him as a child of God, but in II Timothy 3:17 (Amplified New Testament) we see that God has made provision for the child of God to mature into a "man of God, . . . complete and proficient, well-fitted and thoroughly equipped for every good work." God's desire is that His enemies should become His children, and that His children should become His men, and that His men should be mature!

In recent years I have had a rapidly-growing conviction that many of God's children remain in spiritual babyhood, and fail to become mature men, and I feel sure that you have observed similar tendencies. This is a tragic situation, and diametrically opposed to all that God has planned, and not only so, but the purposes of God for His men must inevitably be thwarted when His men insist on remaining in infancy. God knows that unless His children mature into His men, they will be constantly suffering from childish ailments; the Church of God will be exclusively occupied in maintaining her balance (in more ways than one!) and the purposes of God for an un-reached world will be limited.

There are many reasons why God's children do not develop in the way that He expects and desires. These reasons have been dwelt upon at great length on many occasions, but I feel that there is one basic reason that is often overlooked — ignorance! The truth concerning many of God's children is that they are completely ignorant of what God's kind of maturity really is, and naturally they have no working knowledge of the principles under which this maturity can become daily experience. Never let it be said that we are ignorant of these vital issues when Scripture presents them so clearly. "His intention was the perfecting and the full equipping of the saints (His consecrated people), (that they should do) the work of ministering toward building up Christ's body (the Church), that it might develop until we all attain oneness in the faith, and in the comprehension of the full and accurate knowledge of the Son of God; that we might arrive at really *mature manhood* — the completeness of personality which is nothing less than the standard height of Christ's own perfection — *the measure of the stature of the fullness of Christ*, and the completeness found in Him" (Ephesians 4:12, 13, Amplified New Testament). What thrilling, challenging words!

"The measure of the stature of the fullness of Christ" — nothing more and nothing less. This is God's plan for *every* child of His. It may be argued that this kind of maturity can only be realized in Heaven when we meet the Saviour face to face, and are finally delivered from this sinful world, and of course, in one sense this is perfectly true, but do please note carefully that the context of the quotation shows without doubt that this is God's plan *today, here, on this very earth.* "So then, we may no longer be children, tossed (like ships) to and fro between chance gusts of teaching and wavering with every changing wind of doctrine, (the prey of) the cunning and cleverness of unscrupulous men, (gamblers engaged) in every shifting form of trickery in inventing errors to mislead. Rather, *let our lives* lovingly express truth in all things — speaking truly, dealing truly, living truly. Enfolded in love, *let us grow up* in every way and in all things unto Him, Who is the Head, (even) Christ, the Messiah, the Anointed One" (Ephesians 4:14, 15, Amplified New Testament). These verses are an application of the principle outlined in verses 12 and 13 and prove that "the measure of the stature of the fullness of Christ" is the degree of maturity God is expecting to see in His children on His earth in these days!

It may be that you do not find these words either challenging or thrilling, but rather crushing and discouraging. May I suggest that if that is the case, you have not yet discovered the secrets of God, which He is ready to unlock for you in order to reveal how *you* may become a mature man!

2

Big Babies

IT IS NOTHING SHORT OF A TRAGEDY WHEN A BABY FAILS to develop. Some years ago in Germany I visited a hospital for people so retarded in physical and mental development, that their lives could only be described as tragic mis-representations of all that life could and should be.

Men and women born of God, rich in Christ, blessed beyond their wildest dreams, who have failed to develop normally into the "measure of the stature of the fullness of Christ," are tragic mis-representations of all that life in Christ could and should be. Paul reminiscing about his childhood days said, "When I was a child, I spake as a child, I understood as a child, I thought as a child; but when I became a man, I put away childish things" (I Corinthians 13:11). This verse helps to define what childish behavior really is, and we do well to bear in mind, of course, that childish behavior in an adult is irrefutable evidence of immaturity.

A child engages in childish talk — "I spake as a child." The early attempts of children to conquer grammatical intricacies can be both endearing and amusing, and children can often be remarkably adept and informative in their role as conversationalists, but invariably their topics are of limited depth and range. The Lord stated, "Out of the abundance of the heart, the mouth speaketh," and it is perfectly true that topics dear to the heart, are usually near to the lips! Therefore, by carefully measuring and evaluating the depth and scope of spiritual conversation, it is easy to determine the depth of maturity of the spiritual conversationalist. Solemn thought!

A child entertains childish thoughts — "I thought as a child." Childhood is rich in day-dreams, fantasies and vivid imaginations, but adulthood has little time or place for such extravagancies. Life is real and life is earnest! For Christians, the realm of thought life can often be full of childish ideas at the expense of adult spiritual realities.

"For the rest, brethren, whatever is true, whatever is worthy of reverence and is honourable and seemly, whatever is just, whatever is pure, whatever is lovely and lovable, whatever is kind and winsome and gracious, if there is any virtue and excellence, if there is anything worthy of praise, *think on and weigh and take account of these things — fix your minds on them*" (Philippians 4:8, Amplified New Testament). There is no shortage of food for thought here, and presumably as this is the Scriptural catalogue of suitable topics for adult thinking, anything less than this is childish and betrays spiritual immaturity.

A child enjoys childish things. It has been facetiously said that when Christmas morning arrives, it is father who enjoys the model railway, but generally adults find the things of childhood trivial and dissatisfying. In the light of eternity, material things must be defined as trivial and dissatisfying and experience has proved a thousand times that the soul of man can only be satisfied when filled with the things of God. When a child of God becomes enraptured with material things to the detriment of spiritual things, that child of God is betraying a love for the childish, and a disregard for the adult — a fatal attraction for the carnal and a foolish neglect of the spiritual — which can only be regarded as immaturity.

An examination of the epistles of Paul will reveal to even the most casual reader that the Early Church had her share of undernourished and undeveloped children, and it is of prime importance that we should learn today from their experience, and also understand the way in which God regards and deals with this condition.

"For even though by this time you ought to be teaching others, you actually need someone to teach you over again the very first principles of God's Word. You have come to need milk, not solid food. For every one who continues to feed on milk is obviously inexperienced and unskilled in the doctrine of righteousness, (that is, of conformity to the divine will in purpose, thought and action), for he is a mere infant — not able to talk yet! But solid food is for full-grown men, for those whose senses and mental faculties are trained by practice to discriminate and distinguish between what is morally good and noble and what is evil and contrary either to divine or human law" (Hebrews 5:12-14, Amplified New Testament). The charge here is as clear as day. Boundless blessings, untold opportunities and precious hours had been wasted by the Hebrew Christians, because instead of being "full-grown men" (v. 14) they were "mere infants" (v. 13). *Irresponsibility* is the dominant thought.

Irresponsibility in teaching — "You ought to be teaching others" (v. 12). The final command of the Lord was, "Go ye therefore and *teach* all nations . . ." (Matthew 28:19), and years later the aging Paul wrote, "The things that thou hast heard of me among many witnesses, the same commit thou to faithful men, who shall be able to teach others also" (II Timothy 2:2). How wonderfully many Christians obeyed the command, and joyfully, willingly, and effectively taught others what they themselves had experienced of Christ. The "men" covered immense areas with the Gospel of the Risen Christ, while the "babies" were irresponsible, and had neither interest nor part in the active spread of the Message of Life. Praise God for those who today are "men," and pray God for those who remain "babies"!

Irresponsibility in learning — "You actually need someone to teach you over again the very first principles of God's Word" (v. 12). "Take my yoke upon you and *learn* of me," said the Master (Matthew 11:29). Paul said, "I have *learned* how to be content" (Philippians 4:11, Amplified New Testament) and he exhorted, "in understanding be men" (I Corinthians 14:20). The ministry of God's Word to a soul is a priceless gift of God which is abused if treated irresponsibly. The school of experience had vital lessons for Paul, and has for us, but remember that the lessons of experience are valueless if they are not learned and applied. An old schoolmaster of mine continually told me, "Learn by making mistakes, but never make the same mistakes twice." To have the benefit of first-class teaching and to fail to learn is rank irresponsibility.

Irresponsibility in studying — "Everyone who continues to feed on milk is obviously unskilled in the doctrine of righteousness" (v. 13). The Bible is God's Word to man. It is still the world's best seller, but unfortunately it is also the world's least-read best seller. There is absolutely no excuse for a child of God who has God's Word *in his hand*, failing to make absolutely certain that this finds a resting place *in his heart*. "Thy word have I hid in mine heart, that I might not sin against thee" (Psalm 119:11). "Let the word of Christ dwell in you richly in all wisdom" (Colossians 3:16). There is only one method of doing this — by reading, marking, learning, and inwardly digesting. It is interesting to notice that it was to the Hebrews that the oracles of God were committed (Romans 3:2), yet it was these same people who were charged with getting no further than the "first principles" of the oracles of God. The Hebrews had much to answer for in their irresponsible use of the Living Word which had been committed to them, and perhaps the same is true of us! "All Scripture is given by inspiration of God, and is profitable . . ." (II Timothy 3:16), but only if it is studied reverently and regularly!

✳ "However, brethren, I could not talk to you as to spiritual (men), but as to nonspiritual (men of the flesh, in whom the carnal nature predominates), as to mere infants (in the new life) in Christ — unable to talk yet! I fed you with milk, not solid food, for you were not yet strong enough (to be ready for it); but even yet you are not strong enough (to be ready for it) . . ." (I Corinthians 3:1,2, Amplified New Testament). Here again we have the distinction drawn between "spiritual men" and "mere infants." *Inability* is the key thought!

Inability to talk — "unable to talk" (v. 1). With what anticipation parents await the first word to fall from junior's lips! Eventually it comes, and proud parents exult to the neighborhood, "Junior said 'Boo'!" There is nothing unusual about this, but there would be cause for alarm if junior never reproduced a single "Boo" before the age of 21! The Corinthians had had the benefit of Paul's personal teaching, encouragement, and exhortation for eighteen solid months, and the result was that they were still unable to talk! Compare them with the Thessalonians who had the benefit of Paul presence for "three Sabbaths" (Acts 17:2) and yet from them "sounded out the Word of the Lord, not only in Macedonia and Achaia, but also in every place your faith to God-ward is spread abroad" (I Thessalonians 1:8). What a contrast!

Jeremiah said, "Ah, Lord God! Behold I cannot speak; for I am a child," but the Lord said, "Say not I am a child, for thou *shalt* go to all that I shall send thee, and whatsoever I command thee, thou *shalt* speak. Be not afraid of their faces for *I am* with thee" (Jeremiah 1:6-8), and later, "Behold, I have put my words in thy mouth" (Jeremiah 1:9), and in Jeremiah 5:14, "I will make my words in thy mouth fire!" So often the man who says he *cannot* talk, merely means he *will* not talk, because God said, "Open thy mouth wide, and I *will* fill it!" On the basis of this promise, we must believe that the onus is upon God to fill what we are prepared to open wide, and if our lips and mouths are not filled to the full with messages for the King, then it must be because we have not opened wide in simple faith and obedience! The adult who cannot talk is immature indeed.

Inability to digest — "I fed you with milk not solid food, for you were not yet strong enough (to be ready for it)." Most fully grown men would object violently if their wives served them with baby food, but other men have digestive difficulties and have to be satisfied with a childlike diet. Undoubtedly, there are Christians today who suffer from spiritual digestive maladies. They continually enjoy spiritual feasts, but their digestive organs fail to work, with the result, "The Word preached did not profit them not being mixed with faith" (Hebrews 4:2). Jesus said to His disciples,

"If ye know these things happy are ye if ye *do* them" (John 13:17). The digestive organs, which must operate upon the food of God's Word, are faith and obedience, and if they do not operate, the child of God will choke over the Word, and be made sick by the Word. Growth in such circumstances is impossible, and immaturity must be the result. "For as long as (there are) envying and jealousy and wrangling and factions among you, are you not unspiritual and of the flesh, behaving yourselves after a human standard and like mere (unchanged) men? For when one says, I belong to Paul, and another, I belong to Apollos, are you not (proving yourselves) ordinary (unchanged) men?" (I Corinthians 3:3, 4). Despite the miracle of regeneration which had taken place in every one of the Corinthian saints, their lives just did not harmonize. *Incompatibility* was the watchword.

Incompatibility in personal relationships. The petty squabbles, jealousies and envyings of children usually disappear as quickly as they appear, but when the Lord's children engage in such things, untold harm is done, and the repercussions are far-reaching in the extreme. Many a mission station has foundered on the rocks of incompatibility, and many a Church has split on the same razor-edged barrier. Naturally, we must allow for differences of personality, and recognize that incompatibility is the devil's masterpiece. As long as he can persuade the Lord's children to fight each other instead of fighting him, he is delighted, but we must heed the Word of the Lord, "This is my commandment, that ye love one another, as I have loved you" (John 15:12), and we will do well to remember that, according to Galatians 5:19-21, squabbles, jealousies and envyings come from the identical source, and are listed in the same category as murders, adulteries and here-

sies. The attempted work and witness of the Church
of Jesus Christ is ludicrous in some instances, because
those who hold positions of mature authority engage
in activities of juvenile stupidity!

Incompatibility in denominational relationships —
". . . I am of Paul; and another, I am of Apollos . . ."
The Corinthians who could not talk or teach were,
with remarkable inconsistency, extremely voluble when
the subject of partisan loyalties was raised. Church
loyalty, local responsibility, doctrinal certainty are all
of the utmost importance, and must be cherished, but
denominational bigotry should not be tolerated under
any circumstances. "There is *one* body, and *one* Spirit,
even as ye are called in *one* hope of your calling; *one*
Lord, *one* faith, *one* baptism, *one* God and Father of
all, who is above *all*, and through *all*, and in you *all*"
(Ephesians 4:4-6). The deep longing of the Lord Jesus
was "That they may be one" (John 17:21). If the
energy and resources dissipated in internal skirmishes
could be invested in external assaults on devil-held
territory, the individual Christian and the corporate
body of Christ would inevitably demonstrate to a keen-
ly critical world the type of maturity that God en-
visages. However, if denominational incompatibilty is
to be the watchword, we can expect to make little
or no impression on the outside world, and we must
recognize the condemnation in God's Word, that this
sort of thing is childish! "Let us therefore follow after
the things which make for peace and things wherewith one may edify another" (Romans 14:19).

"So then, we may no longer be children, tossed
(like ships) to and fro between chance gusts of teaching, and wavering with every changing wind of doctrine, (the prey of) the cunning and cleverness of unscrupulous men, (gamblers engaged) in every shifting

form of trickery in inventing errors to mislead" (Ephesians 4:14, Amplified New Testament). Ephesus had its shocking, rocking saints, and the Spirit-guided pen of Paul pin-pointed their *instability*.

Instability in daily living — "Tossed like ships." Sundays can be glorious when the Word lives, the sun shines, and the choir boys sing like angels, but Monday can be grim when the boss roars, and the rain pours, and the secretaries chatter like parrots! In one easy movement the unstable saint sinks from the crest of the wave to the trough, and flounders until the next wave comes to the rescue. The Negro spiritual says, "Sometimes I'm up, sometimes I'm down . . ." but the Bible says, "Be ye stedfast, unmoveable, always abounding in the work of the Lord . . ." (I Corinthians 15:58).

Instability in doctrinal direction — "Wavering with every changing wind . . ." (v. 14). "Let every man be fully persuaded in his own mind" (Romans 14:5) is the injunction of Scripture. Believe what you know, and know what you believe! The Christian life which continually changes direction with every wind of doctrine owing to unformed and uninformed views, *must* eventually lose itself, and after a rough passage, sink in the watery wastes of uncertainty and doubt.

The younger son in the story recorded in Luke 15: 12-32 is a perfect illustration of the type of Christian we have been considering. *He engaged in childish talk* — "give me . . . give me . . . give me!" *He entertained childish thoughts* — "I want *all* that I am entitled to and I reserve the right to squander it in any way that I choose!" *He enjoyed childish things* — he spent all, wasted his substance and had a riotous life! Despite this, he did not cease to be his father's son for one fraction of a second! His *irresponsibility* was demonstrated in his selfish disregard for father, home and loved ones. His *inability* was clearly shown by the way in which his youthful enterprise finished in a pigsty without a penny in his pocket or a morsel in his stomach. His *incompatibility* resulted in rebellion against his father and the loss of all his so-called friends in the far country, and his varied and checkered career as a dissatisfied son, determined rebel, and defeated and disillusioned pauper, was one long saga of *instability*. However, despite all this, there is one incontrovertible fact — every moment of this wretched existence he had within him the life blood that linked him with the father, the family and the fortune. Obviously he was not living in the good of all that was his by birth, because he failed to *live* in the measure of the stature of a son, and chose rather to *exist* in the measure of the stature of a baby. Did he stay in this condition? No — one day, sitting with the pigs, he did some heart searching and "came to himself." This is the crux of the story — the vital point of transition. He saw himself as he was in the eyes of his father, instead of being blinded by ill-conceived impressions of his importance, ability and success, and as the truth concerning himself flooded his soul, he knew that his only hope was to get back as quickly as possible to the place where he belonged, in fellowship with the father.

The child of God *must* come to himself and accept God's valuation of his life . . . totally unsatisfactory, utterly useless and completely disgraceful! This is the moment of blinding truth, for when a Christian comes to the end of himself, he arrives at the beginning as far as God is concerned.

Broken and defeated, the young son returned to his father (the source of his life) in deep repentance. The language of his heart was, "I am not worthy," and he was quite right, for he *was* completely unworthy. It is important to note that his repentance was real repentance — not only did he repent of the sins that he had committed against heaven, and against his father, but he also repented of himself. He did not only say that *what he had done* was unworthy and disgraceful, but he admitted that *all that he was* was unsatisfactory, and in effect said, "Father, I am a complete dead-loss." Real repentance is infinitely more than being sorry for what *I have done,* but rather recognizing and repudiating all that *I am.* Job said, "I loathe my words and abhor *myself* and repent in dust and ashes" (Job 42:6, Amplified Old Testament). The delight of the father knew no bounds because his love had never abated, and his intentions had never changed, and suddenly all the father's foreordained possibilities for the son were ready to blossom into reality. Such was the delight in the father's heart that the son's suggestion that he should relinquish his family membership and become an odd-job man on the estate was never even voiced! He was the son of the father, he always had been and he always would be, but now he was going to start behaving in a manner that was consistent with his status of sonship.

"Bring forth the best robe," cried the father. "Take away those rags because no son of mine is going to be dressed in such a manner. From this moment on he is going to *look* like my son."

"Put a ring on his hand! This son who has squandered his livelihood, wasted his substance and finished up bankrupt is now going to be entrusted with this ring which will allow him to act on my behalf in the family business. From this moment I authorize him to seal the documents and make decisions, because now this young man is in business. My son, you are going to *labor* like my son."

"Put shoes on his feet, because he will no longer hobble and stumble through life with blistered, bleeding feet, but it is my intention that my son should stride manfully through life. He is going to *live* like my son."

This thrilling transformation was wrought because the unending grace of the father was made available to a son who came to the end of himself, returned to the source of his life, and joyfully appropriated all the riches that were his by right. This is the one and only road to spiritual maturity. The child of God must repent of what he is, acknowledge that he has life from above, because the risen Christ dwells within him, and appropriate all that Christ is and step out to *look, labor* and *live* like a son of God, who is no longer a big baby, but is developing into a mature man.

3

The Fullness of Christ

GOD HAS NO PLANS FOR MANKIND OUTSIDE OF JESUS
Christ, for it is He "who of God is made unto us wisdom and righteousness and sanctification and redemption" (I Corinthians 1:30). Mankind can anticipate no fulfillment of the promises of God outside of Christ. "For as many as are the promises of God, they all find their Yes (answer) in Him" (II Corinthians 1:20, Amplified New Testament). God's presence is forever barred to man outside of Jesus Christ, for Christ is "the way, the truth and the life" and no man cometh unto the Father but by Him. Christ is the center and circumference of all God's dealings with man. It is not surprising, therefore, to discover that Christ is God's pattern for mankind — "the measure of the stature of the fullness of Christ" is God's ideal for His creatures.

When God made man, His expressed intention was, "Let us make man in our image after our likeness" (Genesis 1:26). This intention was implemented and "God created man in his own image, in the image of God created he him" (Genesis 1:27). We know that this image or likeness was broken and marred when man sinned, but God's desire for man to be in His own likeness never changed. Later, Christ came and was "the express image of his (God's) person" (Hebrews 1:3), and thus Christ, as man, was all that man had failed to be. In Christ, God saw all that He had created man to be, and therefore quite logically if God's thwarted intentions for man had never changed and Christ was all that God desired of man, "the measure of the stature of the fullness of Christ" must be God's ideal for man.

God was so thrilled with His *only* Son that He has planned in Him to "bring *many sons* to glory," and Romans 8:29 (Amplified New Testament) says that He still longs that His children might be "molded into the image of His Son (and share inwardly His likeness) that He might become the *first-born of many brethren*." The delight of the Father was the excellence of His Son as He portrayed man in all his intended glory, and the Father's plans for man are that many children might be molded into the image of His Son.

These foreordained plans of God will reach their fulfillment in eternity, but we must never fall into the trap of assuming that Christ-likeness can only be experienced after death, because Scripture says, "And all of us, as with unveiled face (because we) continue to behold and reflect like mirrors the glory of the Lord, are *constantly being transformed* into (His very own) image in ever increasing splendor, and from one degree of glory to another; (for this comes) from the Lord (Who is the) Spirit" (II Corinthians 3:18, Amplified New Testament). Note carefully the verse speaks of "*all* of us," and it says that when the conditions are being fulfilled, we "are *constantly being transformed* into His very Own image." This process is intended to be in operation *now*. It will be seen, therefore, that "the fullness of Christ" is not a subject of purely academic interest, but of immense practical importance for every child of God. Let us therefore examine what Scripture teaches on this subject in order that we might appreciate exactly what God has in mind for each one of us.

John, the aged apostle, was an ideal man under the guidance of the Spirit of God to record an accurate account of the life, death and resurrection of the Lord Jesus Christ. He was a young man when all the incidents occurred, fully alert and active, dearly beloved of the Master, in the closest proximity to Him, a member of the three whose privilege it was to share the inmost secrets of the Lord. It was to John that the crucified Master entrusted His mother, and the same disciple was the first to look into the empty tomb *and believe* that Christ was risen from the dead! He said, "And the Word became flesh and dwelt among us, full of grace and truth; we have beheld His glory, glory as of the only Son from the Father" (John 1:14, R.S.V.). When John said that he and his colleagues "beheld" the glory of the Lord, he chose his vocabulary carefully in order to convey that theirs was no casual passing glance, but rather a careful, three-year long study of the Master. During this period of the closest possible contact, he witnessed the life of Christ, and he explained this life as being glorious — "full of grace and truth." It was the fullness of Jesus Christ that impressed him.

The fullness of Christ was revealed — "we beheld His glory." John had a twofold objective when he wrote his Gospel. First, he related carefully selected incidents from the life of the Lord which clearly demonstrated the wonder of His Person, in order that the reader might arrive at the conclusion that Jesus was indeed the Christ, the Son of God. Second, he wanted his readers, who had arrived at the intellectual conclusion that Jesus was the Christ, the Son of God, to come into vital relationship with Christ, which would result in His risen life being manifested in their daily lives. This, he pointed out, would be their experience on the basis of simple faith in the Person of Jesus Christ. "But these are written, that ye might believe that Jesus is the Christ, the Son of God; and that believing ye might have life through his name" (John 20:31). It will be appreciated therefore that John's Gospel contains a great amount of evidence concerning the fullness of Christ which is invaluable in the study of the One whom God regards as the perfect "mature man."

He was full of grace. Grace is the favor and loving kindness constantly lavished on man by God. God's grace continually flows in rivers of blessing in man's direction and brings all the riches of God's goodness within man's grasp. The grace of God is totally unmerited and often unappropriated. Grace is the evidence of the heart of God yearning and providing for the rebellious and unthankful, and Christ was full of this kind of grace.

One day, the bigoted, religious Jews dragged a wretched adulteress before the Lord, and set her in front of the crowd. Regardless of the appalling embarrassment that they were causing, they quoted the unsavory details of the case, and the punishment laid down by Moses' Law, and then sat back with a smug expression on their faces to see what Christ would do.

He was in an extremely difficult position, because He loved the sinner, and wanted to save her; He honored the Law, and wanted to fulfill it; and He detested the hypocrisy of the scribes, and wanted to expose it. He had come into the world full of grace and truth, and His fullness of grace reached out to the sinful woman and His fullness of truth honored the Law and sought to expose the hypocrisy. It would appear that the grace and truth in Him were completely contradictory and mutually exclusive, but here, He demonstrated His unique fullness. Raising Himself from the ground He said, "He that is without sin among you, let him first cast a stone at her" (John 8:7).

The hypocrites beat a hasty retreat, because the Law of Moses did its condemning, sin-exposing work deep down in their souls, and after a few moments, only the sinful woman was left. He turned to her, and in tender, loving tones He forgave her, and instructed her to walk in newness of life. This was the fullness of Christ in action as He demonstrated superlative qualities of wisdom, strength, tenacity, fearlessness, initiative, and sheer, unmerited grace.

The physical, moral, mental, spiritual agonies of Christ as He was crucified defy description, and the cursing of the thieves on the adjacent crosses did nothing to alleviate His torment, but He turned and forgave the repentant one. This was a superlative measure of grace. The men who drove the nails through His hands and feet were not resisted, challenged, defied or condemned by the Lord Jesus, but in amazing grace He prayed for them, that they might experience God's forgiveness. He was full of grace.

Grace is that all-sufficient supply that God makes available to every saint. "And God is able to make all grace abound toward you; that ye, always having all sufficiency in all things, may abound to every good work" (II Corinthians 9:8).

One day the Master and His disciples were confronted with 5,000 men and their families who were hungry. He turned to Philip, with, I suspect a smile playing round the corners of His mouth, and said,

"Whence shall we buy bread that these may eat?" (John 6:5), but "He knew what He would do" (John 6:6). Philip, practical and powerless, made calculations, examined possibilities, and quickly admitted defeat. Andrew, active and apologetic, dashed around, did his best, found five loaves and two fishes, and then began to feel rather stupid. Looking rather embarrassed, he said to the Master, "But what are they among so many?" and the Lord answered this question in a most dramatic fashion. In *His* hands, five loaves and two fishes were *more than enough*, and He underlined the lesson by giving each disciple a basketful of bread to carry away. Never for one moment was the Master taken unawares. Not for one moment was He lacking in ability to be Master of the situation. This was His all-sufficiency which was simply God-given grace in abundant measure filling His life at all times. This was His fullness.

He was full of truth. One definition of truth quoted in the *New Bible Dictionary* is "that which really *is* in the absolute sense." Truth is *reality* as opposed to all that is false, unreliable, nebulous, or undefined. Jesus said, "*I am* the Truth" (John 14:6). He claimed that all basic realities were centered and demonstrated in His Person. Bewildered Pilate looked Jesus full in the face and asked, "What is truth?" (John 18:38), not knowing that the Answer was standing just two or three feet in front of him. The truth about life and the truth about God had completely eluded the Roman procurator, and yet the Lord Jesus Christ standing before him was the Living Answer to his bewilderment.

He was the Truth about God. Philip said, "Show us the Father and it sufficeth us" (John 14:8). The Lord answered, "He that hath seen me hath seen the

Father." Christ was the Reality of God's Person, the means whereby the Infinite God made Himself recognizable to finite man. In Christ, the Invisible God became visible; the Intangible God, tangible; the Unapproachable God, approachable. Man need look no further than Christ in his search for the reality of God. When Christ demonstrated love and grace, it was the love and grace of the Invisible God in action.

The merchants in the temple felt the sting of His whip and smarted under the reality of God's wrath against their sin as it was released through Christ. The demons experienced the power of Christ, but knew that they were confronted with the power of the Almighty God through Him, and the elements acknowledged His control, because Christ was the Reality about God. In these days, so many people are puzzled about the Person of God and His attributes, but there is no reason why they should be, because all they need to do is to examine carefully the Person of Jesus Christ, and His claims to be the Truth about God, and they will see God manifested in the flesh.

If, at any moment, Jesus Christ had failed to be about His Father's business, or in any situation had failed to depend implicitly upon the Father who dwelt within Him, the image of God would have been marred, and the Truth about God would have been perverted. The wonderful thing about the life of "the Man Christ Jesus" was that every step of the way was taken in complete abandonment to the Father, and therefore every step of the way was a demonstration of the truth of God. This was His fullness.

He was the Truth about life. Many and varied are the man-made philosophies of life, and Jesus Christ blew most of them sky-high. Unbiased thinkers say that the life of Jesus Christ was outstanding, and usually the most biased people have to admit that His life was unique, whereas the child of God knows full well that the life of Jesus Christ was life lived as life is intended to be lived. In other words, Jesus Christ Himself was the Reality about life, and that of course was what He claimed. "I am the Life" (John 14:6).

The contrast between man's philosophy of life and Christ's principle of life is startling in the extreme. "For all that is in the world, the lust of the flesh, and the lust of the eyes, and the pride of life, is not of the Father, but is of the world. And the world passeth away, and the lust thereof; but he that doeth the will of God abideth for ever" (I John 2:16, 17). These two verses give a summary of the philosophy of God-less man. "The lust of the flesh" means *passion;* "the lust of the eyes" means *possession*, and "the pride of life" means *position*.

Man has not altered very much from New Testament days, because the basic principle of life for many men is that they must be allowed to indulge in their *passions*, without interference from anyone or anything, they must be allowed to heap to themselves *possessions* for their own selfish gratification, and then they will be perfectly affable, friendly and delightful members of society provided that their *position* is maintained. Scripture flatly condemns this principle, and points out that a life lived on this basis is a life of delusion, because these things are of the world, and "the world passes away." Therefore, a life lived for *passion, possession* and *position* (the world's principle which will pass away and disappear) is guaranteed to end in empty, hollow and barren delusion.

Now, look at the principle of life that the Lord Jesus Christ preached: "Verily, verily, I say unto you, Except a corn of wheat fall into the ground and die, it abideth alone; but if it die, it bringeth forth much fruit. He that loveth his life shall lose it; and he that hateth his life in this world shall keep it unto life eternal" (John 12:24, 25). Jesus said that if you want to live, you must die to your passions, possessions and position, and live unto God. He said that if you want to live you must be prepared to abandon and throw away all that you have and are in His direction.

He pointed out that the selfish grain that refuses to die remains alone, but the grain that is prepared to die will automatically and inevitably reproduce a superlative quality and quantity of life. This is the truth about life which Jesus preached and practiced.

There was not one moment in His life when Jesus Christ was not prepared to be 100 per cent expendable and available to the Father, and no one can ever suggest that the principle failed in His life. Two thousand years ago He died and rose again, and the world has Christ to thank for untold blessings, social and spiritual, which still make tremendous repercussions on the twentieth century. Touch His life, His words and His works at any point, under any circumstances, and you will find truth and reality which will bear the most critical examination, and leave you with the irrefutable conclusion that Christ was full of truth and reality in every respect.

He was full of glory. Jesus ignored the s.o.s. from His beloved friends, Mary and Martha, because *He loved them.* This was a strange way of showing His love. The result was that Lazarus died, because the Master, who had it within His power to heal him, allowed him to die. He knew all about the illness, and even though He was miles away from the place where the dead man lay, He was completely Master of the situation. The reason that He gave for the incident was "this sickness is not to end in death, but on the contrary, it is to honor God and to promote His glory, that the Son of God may be glorified through (by) it" (John 11:4, Amplified New Testament).

If Jesus had gone post haste to the sick bed of His beloved friend and healed him, He would once again have proved that He was the great healer. This was not His intention, for He wanted to show man the greatness and fullness of His glory as the "resurrection and the life." To this end, the stage was set for a mighty demonstration of His glory and power. He stood outside the tomb, thanked the Father for what was going to happen, and "shouted with a loud voice, 'Lazarus, come out!' And out walked the man who had been dead . . ." (John 11:43, 44, Amplified New Testament). This was a most telling illustration of the exceeding greatness of His power and the abundance of His glory. Lazarus came forth bound, and it was wonderful to see that the life was there, even if it was limited by graveclothes, but the Lord Jesus then commanded that he should be *loosed* and *let go*. The result was that many believed, but the Jews were antagonized and sought to put Lazarus to death. I suppose few men have had the experience of Lazarus who was the object of murderous intentions within a few moments of being raised from the dead! There was division about Jesus Christ, but one thing was undeniable — Lazarus was alive as a result of the power of the Lord, and His glory was unmistakable.

When the Lord Jesus Christ performed His first miracle in Cana of Galilee and provided the wine for the wedding feast, John summarized the event with the words: "He manifested forth His glory," or, as the *Am-*

plified New Testament says, ". . . by it He displayed
His greatness and His power openly . . ." (John 2:11).
To have made wine from water was a glorious achieve-
ment, but to have made a superlative quality of wine,
as the manager of the feast said He did, was to demonstrate a superlative abundance and fullness of glory.
He was *full* of glory.

He was full of purpose. Jesus always knew where
He was going. He was never at a loss, and was always
driven by an inner power which kept Him to a divine
time-table. He was born "in the fulness of time" (Galatians 4:4), moved at the right speed, and did not die
until "His hour was fully come," and even then it was
He who dismissed His spirit and announced, "It is
finished" — not one minute ahead of schedule, and not
one minute late. His first recorded words were, "I
must be about my Father's business," and His last recorded words before His death were, "It is finished,"
and all that went between was full of purpose.

His attitude was beautifully illustrated in the incident of the blind man. Threatened with cold-blooded
murder through stoning, He passed through the crowd
of would-be assassins, and while He was passing
through, He had time to see a blind beggar. This
blind man did not suspect it, but he was all part of
the timetable, for the Master said, ". . . he was born
blind in order that the workings of God should be
manifested, displayed and illustrated in Him" (John
9:3, Amplified New Testament). Therefore, a few
would-be assassins and stones could not be allowed
to interfere with a divinely appointed timetable, and
the Master knew this. The purpose of God for Him
at that moment was new sight for a blind man, and
spiritual illumination for those who would believe as

a result of the miracle and all other things were incidental. He healed the man, and explained, "I must work the works of him that sent me, while it is day: the night cometh when no man can work. As long as I am in the world, I am the light of the world" (John 9: 4, 5).

The Master had a *sense of commission* which He never forgot. "Him that sent me" was His continuous theme, and His mind was full of this purpose. He also had a *sense of compulsion* — "must" was the word that He was continually using with regard to His life work. His mind and His will, His body and His life, were totally abandoned to the mind and will of the Father who had sent Him and He recognized no other possibility than to be full of this sense of compulsion, "I *must* work the works of Him that sent me." All else was irrelevant to Him, because His task was to be God's man, living on God's earth at God's disposal, and He was full of this purpose. This was His fullness.

This study must of necessity be short, and therefore thoroughly inadequate, but I trust that the isolated incidents quoted have shown that Jesus, the Christ, in three short years, manifested the fullness of love, power, purpose, sufficiency, victory, life and Godliness that is comprehensively described as "the fullness of Christ."

The fullness of Christ was recognized — ". . . glory as of the only Son from the Father." One of the strangest aspects of the life of Christ was that on a number of occasions, when He revealed Himself in all His fullness to a group of people, some *responded to* Him, and others *reacted against* Him. It was possible for one man to recognize the revelation of the fullness of Christ for what it was, and for his fellows to fail to see further than the act of fullness, and in all probability attribute it to strength of character or dynamic of personality. The importance of the revelation of His fullness was that it might be recognized, and this revelation was never intended to act as a spectacle to titillate the sensation-seeking appetite of the masses.

John said, "We (actually) saw His glory . . ." (that was the fullness of Christ revealed) "such glory as an only begotten son receives from his father . . ." (John 1: 14, Amplified New Testament) (that was the fullness of Christ being recognized). After careful observation of the phenomena and characteristics of the life of the Master, John attributed His fullness of person to the activity of God within him, and affirmed that His glory was consistent with His claims. Christ said He was God in action, and He proved it, and John recognized the proof.

When one thief recognized the fullness of Christ as God in action through a man, he was ready to receive Christ in all His fullness, but the other thief died unrepentant and unregenerate as far as we know, even though he had witnessed all his partner in crime had witnessed.

The centurion, hardened by many crucifixions, detected a fullness of grace and power in the dying Saviour, and attributed it to the completeness found in God alone, and voiced his convictions — "Truly this man was the Son of God" (Mark 15:39). Yet we have no record that his dice-playing subordinates arrived at the same conclusion.

The adultress was forgiven, but the Pharisees were condemned by the self-same revelation, because she recognized the revelation of His fullness and received Him in all her need, but they failed to recognize the revelation, and went away "dead in trespasses and sins."

The irrefutable evidence of His fullness in action in the resurrection of Lazarus was given a mixed reception — ". . . many of the Jews . . . believed" (John 11:45), but others went to the chief priests and their cronies, with the result that they "took counsel together for to put him to death" (John 11:53).

No man can come into a vital experience of Christ purely by gazing with rapt attention at the Masterly fullness of His life, but he must recognize who Christ is, and be prepared to attribute His fullness to the Father who dwelt within Him.

The fullness of Christ was received — "Out of His fullness we all received . . ." At this point, it might occur to someone to jump to a conclusion which is false. Their thinking might be as follows: The fullness of Christ was revealed and recognized; God expects me to attempt to attain a similar fullness, therefore I must roll up my sleeves, grit my teeth, set my jaw and make a sincere attempt to be like Christ in all His fullness.

This idea, which is all too common, reminds me of the story of a little boy who was given a bantam, and when it laid its first egg, he was terribly disappointed, because the egg was so small, and he did not honestly feel that it was a satisfactory day's work for a hen. Immediately, he bought an ostrich's egg, and kneeling in front of the unsuspecting fowl said, "Have a good look at this, and try harder next time!" Try as it would, the bantam could never lay anything remotely like an ostrich egg, regardless of its sincerity, or all manner of activity, for the simple reason that it just was not built for that sort of thing!

No — the Christian is not to endeavor to emulate the glorious life of Jesus Christ, the Supreme Example, because if he does, he is bound to fail. There is as much chance of a forgiven sinner emulating the fullness of Christ as there was of the little bantam laying an ostrich egg through looking at the supreme example. We are not built for that sort of thing!

John, however, made this point clear, for in John 1:16 (Amplified New Testament) he said, "For out of His fullness (abundance) we all received — all had a share and we were all supplied with — one grace after another and spiritual blessing upon spiritual blessing, and even favor upon favor and gift (heaped) upon gift." The glorious experience of which John spoke is far removed from a sincere attempt to emulate Christ's glorious example. Deep down in his soul he knew what it was to have the fullness of Christ made real within, as grace, spiritual blessing, favor and gift heaped upon gift became his daily experience.

God had *imparted to him* all that He *expected from him,* and all God wanted to see in John was Christ in all His fullness. This is something which many Christians fail to appreciate. God's ideal is not dangled tantalizingly before our eyes like a donkey's carrot, but is invested in us in the person of the indwelling Christ.

A few years ago, I was watching a party of climbers attempting to scale the North Wall of the Eiger, 13,000 feet of sheer rock face, high in the Swiss Alps. The climb is extremely dangerous and totally impossible to all but the most expert climbers. If anyone had challenged me to climb it, or persuaded me to attempt the climb, the result would have been a foregone conclusion—disaster! I would either have slipped and been killed, died from exhaustion or exposure, or expired from sheer fright. As I watched the toiling men, a high-altitude balloon from a nearby exhibition floated past. It quickly ascended the vertical side of the mountain and within a short time appeared to hover over the summit. To me, climbing the Eiger was an impossibility, but ascending to the summit in a balloon was well within my capability! All that was necessary for me to do was to climb into the basket beneath the balloon, throw out the ballast and start moving. In a remarkable way, the gravity-defying properties of the gas-filled balloon would have been imparted to me, and the mountain wall would have been ascended.

The God-defying principle of self and sin in the soul of man can never be cajoled, challenged or commanded to ascend the vertical wall of the fullness of Christ, but the man in whose soul the sin-defying properties of the Risen Christ are made real can constantly be experiencing a series of miracles whereby he is translated into a new strata of spiritual experience. From the first moment when John left his father and family, his boats and his nets to follow the Master, the Lord Jesus started work in the young man's life. A process was put into operation initially by the *external teaching* of the Master as *He walked with* him, and later this process was carried on by the *internal transforming* of the Master as He *lived within* him.

God, in His goodness, allowed John a long life before he penned the fourth Gospel, and it is of vital importance to note that it was over this long period that John had tested and experienced the fullness of Christ in daily living. When John said that the fullness of Christ was received, he was giving a word of personal testimony which cannot be refuted, and which we do well to believe. He had labored in Jerusalem and Ephesus in the fullness of Christ, he had been exiled in Patmos in the same fullness and he had known what it was to counter the untold sorrow of his brother's martyrdom in the power of the all-sufficient, indwelling Saviour. Regardless of the geographical location or changing situation, he had continually drawn upon the fullness of Christ. A careful examination of the facts concerning John demonstrate in a wonderful way what it meant in John's experience to be transformed into "the measure of the stature of the fullness of Christ," because he had received all that Christ is.

At the first the Lord gave him the surname "Son of Thunder" (Mark 3:17, Amplified New Testament), presumably because of his violent disposition, and his uncontrollable rage. John was a *violent* man. As an old man on Patmos, he was "in the spirit on the Lord's day" (Revelation 1:10), a far cry indeed from the days when young Boanerges was often in a temper in the Lord's way. He became a *gracious, spiritual* man.

John felt that he would like to have the top seat in the Kingdom and he had no compunction in bringing his request to the Master. "They said unto him, Grant unto us that we may sit, one on thy right hand, and the other on thy left hand, in thy glory" (Mark 10:37). The young man, of course, was of the opinion that he was the ideal person to occupy the seat of highest honor.

John was a *proud* man. In I John 3:16 (Amplified New Testament) he said, "We ought to lay our lives down for those who are our brothers in Him" — a striking transformation from the days when he looked upon his brethren as people who had a habit of getting in his way, disrupting his well-laid plans and competing with him for the place of pre-eminence. He became a *humble, self-effacing* man.

John was a *hard* man. When the Samaritan villages had little or no time for the Master as He traveled to Jerusalem, John made a personal request for the immediate destruction of the offending neighborhood, but the Lord rebuked him. "But he turned, and rebuked them, and said, Ye know not what manner of spirit ye are of" (Luke 9:55). These Samaritan villages became the scene of his own gracious ministry in later years. Instead of calling down fire and brimstone, he prayed down untold blessing. "Now when the apostles which were at Jerusalem heard that Samaria had received the word of God, they sent unto them Peter and John: who, when they were come down, prayed for them, that they might receive the Holy Ghost" (Acts 8:14, 15). He became a *concerned* man.

John was an *intolerant* man. The man who was exorcising demons without having first become a member of the disciples' fellowship caught the sharp edge of John's tongue. "And John answered and said, Master, we saw one casting out devils in thy name; and we forbad him, because he followeth not with us. And Jesus said unto him, Forbid him not: for he that is not against us is for us" (Luke 9:49, 50). Years rolled by before he wrote in I John 1:7 (Amplified New Testament) "But if we (really) are living and walking in the Light as He (Himself) is in the light, we have *true, unbroken fellowship with one another* . . ." He became a *loving* man.

Instead of violence, intolerance, pride and bitterness, now read peace, joy, love and blessing, and take John at his word as he attributed this remarkable transformation in his life to the outworking of the indwelling fullness of the Risen Christ.

This testimony of John's is in vivid contrast to so many testimonies one hears from the Lord's people in these days: "I was saved so many years ago — I have often failed Him, but He has never failed me, and I am looking forward to being with Him one day." The testimony that God longs to hear is that the Lord Jesus is filling, flooding, transforming, and revolutionizing our lives by His Own gracious activity within, and as a result we are growing up into "the measure of the stature of the fullness of Christ."

4

The Fullness of Life

"HOW WONDERFUL IT MUST HAVE BEEN FOR JOHN THE Apostle"; "If only I could have an experience like him"; "Why doesn't this happen to me?" Sometimes this is the yearning, bewildered heart language of God's children. Whenever this type of thinking finds an expression in words, the child of God concerned betrays a fatal lack of spiritual understanding. No one living in this day and age need assume that by being born in the twentieth century, they are automatically at a disadvantage compared with John and the other apostles.

True, John had many precious experiences as he reclined on the Master's breast, asked personal questions, and beheld His glory, but do remember that none of these experiences in themselves made much difference to his life, because in the garden, he slept, at the trial, he kept his distance, at Calvary, he fled, and in the Upper Room, he trembled. It was after all these events that things began to happen in his life.

When the day of Pentecost arrived, he was with the other disciples and the Spirit of God came upon them all. The result, we are told, was that they ceased to become individual members of an organization, and they became integral parts of a living organism — the body of Christ. Before the day of Pentecost, the disciples went their several ways, did their best, and usually failed, but on the great day, they were all baptized into one body. They became vitally united to Christ, and to each other, and immediately the world became aware of them.

Now I Corinthians 12:13 (Amplified New Testament) says, "For by (means of the personal agency of) one (Holy) Spirit we were all, whether Jews or Greeks, slaves or free, baptized (and by baptism united together) into one body, and all made to drink of one (Holy) Spirit." It is evident from a study of the historical record that it was being baptized into one body and drinking of One Spirit that did the trick in the lives of the disciples. The importance of this to us is that the verse says, "*We were all* baptized into *one body*.*" Glorious news indeed that we, in the twentieth century, are members of the same body, partakers of the same nature, occupying the same position in the same Christ, and indwelt by the same Spirit as the original Christians. We cannot say that we envy John, or that we need another experience, when God says that the moment we trusted Christ we *were* given all that John and the fellow disciples ever received.

The Word of God states that if you are a Christian, you are "in Christ" and in Colossians 2:10 (Amplified New Testament) it says, "And you are in Him, made full and have come to fullness of life — in Christ you, too, are filled with the Godhead." The stark statement of Scripture is unmistakable — if you are a Christian you are in Christ — if you are in Christ you *are* made full, and if you are in Christ, you *have* come to fullness of life. This poses problems for some people who say, "If that is what a Christian has, I am afraid I haven't got it, therefore I am not a Christian."

We can easily demonstrate that the argument is faulty. "Men marry girls" is a perfectly true statement. A bachelor reading this statement might reason as follows: "Men marry girls, and I did not marry a girl, therefore presumably I am not a man." However, the fact of the matter is that he is a man who did not avail himself of the right of a man to marry a girl, and as a result (in the opinion of some) he has missed quite a large slice of life (although admittedly he has kept quite a large slice of capital!). The answer to the problem of the Christian is exactly the same. If his experience does not match the standard outlined in Scripture, it does not mean that he is not a Christian, but rather that there is a large slice of life of which he is entirely ignorant, and totally lacking.

Let us examine Colossians 2:10 a little more closely: "You are in Him, made full and have come to fullness of life — in Christ you too are filled with the Godhead." This verse is written with divine dogmatism, and allows no evasion or argument. The statement is unequivocal, and is made to be accepted, believed, rejoiced in and experienced. In *Him* you *are* made full. The good news of the Gospel is that in Christ *you are* (potentially) all that God desires, and in Christ, *you have* (potentially) *all* that God has to offer. Note carefully, however, that the abundance of blessing is only available "in Christ." These two small words hold depths of truth that we do well to understand.

THE STATE OF BEING 'IN CHRIST'

The Bible speaks of two major categories of mankind — those who are "in Adam," and those who are "in Christ." When a man is in Adam, God reckons to him all that applied to Adam. Adam rebelled, sinned, died spiritually, and came under the righteous wrath of God, and in God's economy, the man "in Adam" enjoys an identical status and experience. No man has to try very hard to have a rebellious, sinful, Adamic nature — he is

born "in Adam," and therefore automatically born dead
to God, and he is automatically "condemned already."
In the same way, when God says a man is "in Christ,"
this means that He looks upon the man in such a way
that He reckons to him all that Christ is, and regards him
as having experienced all that Christ experienced. The
Scriptures say that we "have been crucified with Him"
(Galatians 2:20), "buried with Him" (Colossians 2:12),
we are "risen with Him" (Colossians 2:12), "brought
to life with Him" (Colossians 2:13, Amplified New
Testament) and "seated in the heavenlies with Him"
(Ephesians 2:6), and as we have already seen, we are
"come to fulness of life in Him." This briefly then is
the state of being "in Christ."

THE STEPS TO BEING 'IN CHRIST'

Ephesians 1:12, 13 outlines four steps whereby a
man "in Adam" can become a man "in Christ." "That
we should be to the praise of his glory, who first trusted
in Christ. In whom ye also trusted, after that ye heard
the word of truth, the gospel of your salvation: in
whom also after that ye believed, ye were sealed with
that holy Spirit of promise." The four steps outlined
are as follows:

1) Hearing the Word of God;
2) Believing the Word of God;
3) Trusting oneself to the Son of God;
4) Being sealed with the Spirit of God.

"Faith cometh by hearing and hearing by the Word
of God" (Romans 10:17), and the man reckoned dead
and condemned in Adam must hear the Word of God.
Having heard the Word of God there are two avenues
open to him — either he can believe or disbelieve — he
can either give an intellectual "yes" or an intellectual
"no" to the Truth as it has been presented to him.

There are people who say that an intellectual appreciation of the facts of the Gospel is all that God requires of man, but this is not so. Having said "yes" intellectually to the message of the Gospel, the man "in Adam" must then act upon what he has learned, and trust himself to the One of whom he has learned. Immediately when he does this he is sealed with the Holy Spirit and is stamped as belonging to God — reserved by God for eternity and from that moment he is "in Christ." The man who has taken the first three steps and automatically experienced the fourth step is "in Christ," and according to the Word of God, he *has* come to fullness of life whether he realizes it or not.

THE SIGNIFICANCE OF BEING 'IN CHRIST'

A child born in a royal palace will have little conception of the deep significance of his birth. Nevertheless, despite his lack of appreciation, the crown, the kingdom and the throne are his by right from the moment of birth. The same is true of the man born into Christ — the crown, the Kingdom and the throne are his from the moment of new birth.

Ephesians 1 is full of teaching about all the royal splendors reckoned to a man "in Christ," so let us spend a few moments looking into the chapter.

1) In Him we are *received* — "accepted in the beloved" (Ephesians 1:6). In Adam, a man is rejected and condemned, but in Christ he is received and welcomed as a member of the family. As far as God is concerned he is as welcome in the Father's presence as the Son Himself. A man who insists on trying to enter the divine presence in the rags of his own self-righteousness is automatically destined to summary ejection. It is only in Christ that a man is clothed in the right manner for the Royal Presence.

2) In Him we are *redeemed* — "in whom we have redemption" (Ephesians 1:7). Bound by sin, blighted in life, barren and hopeless as a slave in a slave market — this is the condition of a man "in Adam." Christ, the Great Emancipator, came down to the slave market to pay the price of liberation in order that the chains might be snapped, and the slaves set free to enjoy the glorious liberty of the sons of God. This is what it means to be redeemed, and this is the heritage of all who are "in Christ" — they are set free to be His slaves. The price that Christ paid for the redemption of man was His own life, His precious blood, Calvary, being made sin; the wrath of a Holy God, the tomb, the realm of departed spirits, and His glorious resurrection.

3) In Him we have *remission* — "the forgiveness of sins" (Ephesians 1:7). The man "in Christ" has a clean sheet. The record of his sin has been wiped clean, and God has put his sin "out of sight" (Isaiah 38:17), "out of reach" (Psalm 103:12), "out of memory" (Jeremiah 31:34). There is nothing to answer for, no condemnation, and there is no guilt attached to the forgiven sinner. A man convicted of an offense must serve the sentence passed upon him. When he has served the sentence the Law has no further demands upon him, but on going home, the released prisoner may find that a stigma attaches to him. The neighbors avoid him, his employers dismiss him, and his friends desert him, because of his past record. God recognizes no stigma on the man "in Christ," but has graciously forgiven and forgotten all his sin, and made him just as if he had never sinned.

4) In Him we are *reserved* — "that in the dispensation of the fulness of time He might gather together in one all things in Christ" (Ephesians 1:10). The man "in Christ" need have no fears for the future

or qualms (for himself) as he surveys the world situation because "in Christ" he has been reserved by God for the final triumphal day in glory, and no wars or bombs, famines or tribulations can ever touch his reserved position "in Christ."

5) In Him we are *rich* — "blessed be the God and Father of our Lord Jesus Christ who *hath blessed us* with all spiritual blessings in heavenly places in Christ" (Ephesians 1:3). The brief summary of the blessings "in Christ" given above is intended as a background to this glorious verse which confirms all that we have considered thus far. Notice carefully the tense of the verse. The man "in Christ" *has been blessed,* and this means an accomplished fact — something which has already occurred in the past experience of the man "in Christ." Notice also the scope of the words — *"every spiritual blessing* in the heavenly realm" (Ephesians 1:3, Amplified New Testament). A man "in Christ" is rich indeed, and he may either live in his riches and possess his possessions, or endure a standard of poverty which is totally inconsistent with his true position.

Recently I read of a dirty, unkempt, starving old lady who lived in appalling poverty. One day she was found dead in the pitiful squalor of her own home. The people who made the sad discovery were staggered with other discoveries they made. In the squalid home they found her bank account, her investment records and private hoards of currency, and the truth of her position became apparent. Her poverty was self-imposed and completely contradictory to her true position. There is no excuse for a child of God in Christ, rich beyond his wildest dreams, failing to enjoy anything but God's best which is "the fullness of life in Christ."

Noah illustrates the truth we have been seeking to

emphasize in this chapter, and a study of his story may assist in our appreciation of the doctrine of being "in Christ."

Noah heard the Word of God. One day God met Noah and told him the truth about mankind — "every imagination of the thoughts of his heart was only evil continually" (Genesis 6:5), and the truth about Himself, "And it repented the Lord that he had made man on the earth, and it grieved him at his heart" (Genesis 6:6), and also the truth about His intentions — "I will destroy man" (v. 7). Noah listened with awe to the Word of God, and then he heard with tremendous joy, "Make thee an ark." This was the word of salvation which gladdened his heart — the message of hope which burned deeply into his soul.

Noah believed the Word of God. Having listened to the minute details of God's message, Noah had to decide whether he believed or disbelieved what he had been told. He thought the matter over and came to the intellectual conclusion that what he had heard from God was the Truth. He was so convinced that he promptly rolled up his sleeves and his beard, and started to chop down trees! Despite the amused comments of the neighborhood, he carried on building a vast boat without any place to sail it. He was thoroughly convinced of the truth to the extent of being made a fool for what he believed, but note carefully that at that moment he was not saved.

Noah trusted himself to the ark. One day after much chopping, hammering, animal-training and family-organizing, Noah received a gracious invitation from the Lord, "Come thou and all thy house into the ark" (Genesis 7:1). Note that the invitation came from within, for in effect God said, "Come and join Me, Noah." God did not tell Noah to get into the ark, but rather invited him to come into communion with Himself, and any invitation of God is intended to draw a man into a vital experience of Himself. Noah had two more alternatives — either he could act upon what he believed to be the truth, or he could continue to believe, but do nothing about it. The sky was blue, the sun was shining, the crowd was jeering, and the voice of the Lord was ringing in his heart. A battle ensued, but the Lord won. Noah stepped into the ark, and to apply a New Testament parallel, immediately he was "in ark" (Genesis 7:7).

Noah was sealed by God. He entered the ark, and salvation was his — a salvation that far exceeded his wildest dreams. To reserve it all for him, "The Lord shut him in" (Genesis 7:16). He was sealed, locked in with God, destined to untold blessings. When the judgment fell, it fell on the ark, and Noah was saved, while those who remained outside the ark were lost. For over a year Noah cruised in his ark, rejoicing in the goodness of God, and the greatness of his salvation. One day the ark hit a rock and rested on Mount Ararat. Noah had drifted and rejoiced, but now another phase of his salvation was to be unfolded. After some time "Noah removed the covering of the ark, and looked . . ." (Genesis 8:13).

Noah looked out — ". . . and, behold the face of the ground was dry" (Genesis 8:13). For months he had looked out of the ark and seen nothing but sea and sky. Both were heavy with the evidence of God's judgment against sin. Perhaps on occasions he had looked forward to being delivered from this watery, sin-torn, God-judged world, and longed to be in the presence of his God. But now he looked out, and behold, a new land stretched as far as his eyes could see. The child of God who continually looks *back* to a *past salvation* and *on* to a *future salvation* inevitably misses much of God's salvation, because God expects him to look *out* to his *present salvation.* The land is rich and full, packed with potential, and inviting instant exploration.

A *retrospective* look is rich and delightful, and the Lord commanded His children to partake regularly of the bread and the wine in remembrance of Him. An *introspective* look is necessary, for the Lord would have us remember what we are—nothing—and the Scripture commands, "Let a man examine himself." Remember, however, that morbid introspection is not God's plan for His children. A *prospective* look is glorious and Scriptural — "Looking for the blessed hope and glorious appearing of the great God and our Saviour Jesus Christ" (Titus 2:13), but God does not want His children looking *on* to the exclusion of looking *out.*

There is a danger in spending so much time examining "the signs of the times" that the examiners have no time to live *in the times,* and experience His fullness *in* these times. An *extraspective* (if there is not such a word, there should be!) look is vitally important. II Corinthians 5:17 (Amplified New Testament) says, "Therefore if any person is (ingrafted) in Christ, the Messiah, he is (a new creature altogether,) a new creation; the old (previous moral and spiritual condition) has passed away. *Behold, the fresh and new has come.*" "In Christ" the old *has passed away,* so there is not a lot of point in gazing on what God says has gone, but rather, "Behold, the fresh and new has come!" Behold! — look out! — the land is characterized by freshness and newness, and depression and boredom are aliens in this land.

Noah stepped out — "Go forth of the ark" (Genesis 8:16). The same Lord who *invited* Noah to *step in,* commanded Noah to *step out.* The new land of rich provision, and full experience is not an "optional extra" to salvation from the penalty of sin. It is an integral part of the only salvation God has to offer. God recognizes no salvation that can blot out the past, save in the eternal future, and yet has nothing to offer for the present. His salvation has three tenses, and all three tenses are to be equally enjoyed. Some stools have three legs, and to function properly all three legs must be of equal length and equal strength. If one leg is missing or is shorter than the other, then the stool is unsatisfactory, and lacking. The three tenses of salvation should have equal strength, and equal application in the life of a Christian, and if one tense is lacking, then the whole Christian experience will inevitably be lop-sided. Often it is the present tense experience that is lacking, for whilst there is a full appreciation of the past salvation (forgiveness of sins) and a glorious anticipation of the future salvation (the translation into His presence) there is no appropriation of the present salvation (the enjoyment of fullness of life in Christ).

The simple faith of Noah which motivated his step in was in evidence as he stepped out. Noah heard the word "go forth," and "Noah went forth" (Genesis 8:18). To him, the one step of faith into the salvation of God was as logical as the series of steps of faith that were going to carry him to the extremities of the riches of a new land which God had made part of his salvation. Noah did not look out and long for the land. He did not have an all-night prayer meeting asking God to make the land his experience. Noah did not sit in his ark giving his testimony of how God had saved him from the flood, and he did not plead with God to come and do a wonderful work in his heart that was going to bring the land to his own experience. He *looked* out, and he *stepped* out.

If Noah had sat in his ark much longer, he would probably have suffered from acute boredom and deep depression, even though he was saved. But once he stepped out, he had no time to be either bored or depressed. The man of God who gets bored or depressed is the man who is still sitting in the ark and rejoicing that his sins are forgiven, but hasn't reached the point of stepping out and exploring the land. Remember, boredom and depression are aliens in the land of freshness and newness.

Noah found out. The land *looked* dry when he *looked out,* but he did not *know* it was dry until he *stood* on it. There is just the possibility that the dry-looking ground might have disintegrated under foot, and he could conceivably have sunk and drowned. The truth of God looks good, but it does not *feel* good until the man of God steps out and commits himself to the truth. A meal can look good, but need not necessarily be good, but as soon as the eater eats he proves its goodness, and in the same way, the promises and provisions of God only operate in response to the faith of a Christian. The degree in which experience corresponds to truth, is always in direct proportion to the degree of faith exercised in the truth. It is impossible to "find out," without "stepping out." Therefore, fullness of life in Christ is only enjoyed through appropriation — "O taste and see that the Lord is good" (Psalm 34:8). Tasting comes first, and seeing comes second, but the Lord *is* good all the time. The goodness of the Lord is only seen when tasted. The thrill of the land is only "found out," when you have stepped out.

Noah gave out. The fullness of life was so great when Noah stepped out, and his joy and gratitude was so deep that the very first thing he did was to give back what had been entrusted to him. "Noah builded an altar unto the Lord . . . and the Lord smelled a sweet savour . . ." (Genesis 8:20, 21). The results of his first step in the fullness of life were tremendous. Through his offering, the man of God was gratified, the heart of God was satisfied, and the name of God was glorified, and he only offered because he had tasted and seen and enjoyed the goodness of God through stepping out and finding out. The man of God who never reaches the point of joyful, thankful abandonment of himself and his means to the gracious God obviously is not experiencing the fullness of Christ, for a man who has "looked out," "stepped out," and consequently "found out" will inevitably be ready to give sacrificially of himself, his time and his assets to the One in whom he has fullness of life.

Noah reached out. The inevitable result of Noah's new life was to be multiplication — "Be fruitful and multiply" (Genesis 9:1). God never intends His blessing to come to a halt in a life, but He invariably imparts blessing *to* an individual in order that the blessing might flow unhindered *through* the individual. Speaking to Abraham, God said, "I will bless thee . . . and thou shalt be a blessing" (Genesis 12:2), and the person living in the fullness of life *expects* to be a blessing to others. Outreach does not have to be organized and encouraged in the life of a man "in Christ" who is enjoying the fullness of life, because outreach will be the inevitable consequence of his enjoyment of all that is his in Christ. So often the Church has a *program* that has to be *pushed* instead of an *experience* that has to be *expressed.*

The story is told of the old vicar who, as he watched the train pass near his vicarage, habitually threw his hat in the air and shouted, "Hallelujah." Questioned by the Bishop about his peculiar behavior he replied,

"Surely I can shout 'Hallelujah' about the train. It is the only thing that moves in my parish without my pushing it." Men never push bullets or encourage arrows. They simply release them and the power inherent within them does the rest. There is no necessity to cajole, persuade or push the man who is living in the fullness of life, for the power inherent within him must result in vital, effective outreach.

Noah stood out. "The fear of you and the dread of you shall be on every beast of the earth . . ." (Genesis 9:2). Noah was to be absolutely unmistakable as he lived in the fullness of life on Mount Ararat. Noah was going to be the one in complete control of his environment. The creatures who lived around him were to recognize that he was the man who "had something." Romans 5:17 (Amplified New Testament) says, "For if, because of one man's trespass (lapse, offense), death reigned through that one, much more surely will those who receive (God's) overflowing grace (unmerited favor) and the free gift of righteousness (putting them into right standing with Himself) reign as kings in life through the One, Jesus Christ, the Messiah, the Anointed One." The overflowing grace, and the free gift of righteousness (that is, all that is entailed in the riches that are ours "in Christ"), when experienced and enjoyed should be translated into an outstanding quality of life recognized by the world and called by God "reigning as kings in life through Jesus Christ."

"In Christ" therefore is the position of every born-again Christian, and in Christ every Christian *has come* to fullness of life. Are you sitting in the ark reflecting, or standing on Ararat rejoicing?

5

Filled and Flooded

IT IS POSSIBLE FOR A CHRISTIAN TO BELIEVE THE DOCtrines of "Union with Christ" and "Position in Christ" and yet to remain remote, aloof, and untouched by the experience of the fullness of Christ which the Bible teaches is the experiential outcome of the doctrines.

I remember some years ago attending a performance of Tchaikovsky's "Pathetique" Symphony, and at first I was completely unmoved and untouched by the music, even though the auditorium in which I was sitting was filled with glorious harmony. Later in the program, however, a remarkable change came over me, for I found my heart soaring with the music, my feet tapping to the rhythm, and at the conclusion of the performance, my hands were clapping in appreciation. Heart, hands, and feet were affected because the music invaded my soul. The difference in attitude and reaction came about when the music ceased to be *all around me*, and managed to get right *into me*.

The teaching of the Scriptures is that we are in Christ — the *realm* of spiritual experience. Scripture also teaches that Christ is in us — the *reality* of Christian experience. The realm of Christian experience is only made reality through the activity of the Lord Jesus Christ Himself living and reigning within the heart of the redeemed sinner. It is when the Lord Jesus gets right *into you* that the heart, hands, and feet move in response to the music of Heaven's realm in which you are seated in Christ.

When Paul prayed for his Ephesian converts, he did so *expecting* God to answer his prayers. His expectations for his sons and daughters were of the most sublime degree imaginable. He told them, "I bow my knees before the Father of our Lord Jesus Christ, For whom every family in heaven and on earth is named — (that Father) from whom all fatherhood takes its title and derives its name. May He grant you out of the rich treasury of His glory to be strengthened and reinforced with mighty power in the inner man by the (Holy) Spirit (Himself) — indwelling your innermost being and personality. May Christ through your faith (actually) dwell — settle down, abide, make His permanent home — in your hearts! May you be rooted deep in love and founded securely on love, That you may have the power and be strong to apprehend and grasp with all the saints (God's devoted people, the experience of that love) what is the breadth and length and height and depth (of it); (That you may really come) to know — practically, through experience for yourselves — the love of Christ, which far surpasses mere knowledge (without experience); that you may be filled (through all your being) unto all the fullness of God — (that is) may have the richest measure of the divine Presence and become a body wholly filled and flooded with God Himself!" (Ephesians 3:14-19, Amplified New Testament). Paul was interested in nothing less than his converts being filled "unto all the fullness of God," and becoming bodies wholly "filled and flooded with God Himself." This, he explained, was only possible when the Christ who lived within them was allowed to "settle down, abide, and make His permanent home" in their hearts. The indwelling

Christ was to be the dynamic whereby they were to experience "the richest measure of the divine Presence."

At this point it may be beneficial to summarize what I trust we have seen so far.

Christ Died —
    The *Prelude* to all Christian Experience.
Christ Lived —
    The *Pattern* of all Christian Experience.
We Live in Christ —
    The *Province* of all Christian Experience.
Christ Lives in Us —
    The *Power* of all Christian Experience.

Now let us look into the Word of God to see what it teaches about the indwelling life of the Lord Jesus and the resultant power outflowing from His presence. The Biblical definition of a Christian is "a person in whom Christ lives." "Examine yourselves, whether ye be in the faith; prove your own selves. Know ye not your own selves, how that Jesus Christ is in you, except ye be reprobates?" (II Corinthians 13:5). A man is a Christian if he has Christ indwelling him, and if Christ is not indwelling him, he is not a Christian. If a man goes through the motions of Christianity without Christ living within, then on the authority of God's Word he is nothing more than a "counterfeit" (II Corinthians 13:5, Amplified New Testament). It is clear that it is the indwelling presence of Christ that differentiates between a Christian and a non-Christian. The indwelling presence of Christ is the basic characteristic of Christianity. The major religions of the world have much teaching, many concepts, numerous precepts but none can offer the indwelling presence of God Himself, who alone can fulfill the concepts and obey the precepts. "For it is God which worketh *in you* both to *will* and to *do* of His good pleasure" (Philippians 2:13). Christianity is Christ living, moving, working, and proving Himself in the hearts of His servants.

CHRISTIANITY *minus* CHRIST *equals* IANITY

and IANITY is only one letter removed from INANITY, which is plain, rank stupidity.

Paul writing to the Colossians said he had been made a minister of the Word of God — the "mystery" which had been hidden from many generations. To the saints, however, God was pleased to reveal the riches of the glory of this mystery, which is *"Christ in you"* (Colossians 1:27). The unknown and unappreciated secret (for this is the literal meaning of "mystery") for generations had been "Christ in you," but God in His goodness has revealed it to mankind in this day of grace. Since the day of Pentecost, the hidden mystery has become an open secret, but unfortunately, the mystery *revealed* to the saints, is still the mystery *concealed* to some saints.

THE REALITY OF HIS INDWELLING

When a sinner receives Christ as his Saviour, he receives *Christ*. It is impossible to separate Christ the Saviour, whom men receive for the forgiveness of their sins, and Christ the Indweller, the power and dynamic of all Christian experience. There is only one Christ and when He is received, *He* is received. This is elementary in the extreme, and yet the reality of this basic elementary teaching is often missed completely. "To as many as received *Him* . . ." (John 1:12). The right to become a son of God is reserved for the person who receives the *person of Christ* and not for the person who is influenced by His teaching or challenged by His example. Jesus promised, "If any man hear my voice and open the door, *I* will come in" (Revelation 3:20).

For many years after I had trusted Christ as my Saviour and had invited Him to come into my heart and life, I did not grasp the simple, stupendous fact that when I received Him, *I* received *Him* — when He came to live in my heart, *He* came to *live* in *me*. The promise of the Word of God is that the sinner who needs Christ and invites Christ to take up residence, will receive a *living* person — Christ. Yet there are many who believe this to be good, sound doctrine, and yet live as if they had received a variety of commodities, rather than the Person promised.

Christ who promised Himself to come through the open door of a repentant heart, did not cheat by pushing in a certificate of forgiveness, a cozy "saved" feeling, a ticket to Heaven, and reservations for eternity, together with a dose of peace and joy to be taken three times daily, or when needed! *He* promised that *He* would come in, and come in *He* did. The reality of His promise speaks of the reality of His Person, and the reality of His Person guarantees the reality of His Presence. Therefore, the question which each Christian must ask is, "Does my Christianity depend upon the living, indwelling Person of the Risen Christ, or upon a set of doctrines, a code of ethics, a set of rules, and a denominational pattern?" "Is my Christianity a demonstration of the reality of His Presence, or purely a rigid adherence to an organized procedure, a firm belief in facts which appear to have little practical relevance to everyday living, and a round of activities which must be kept in motion to preserve appearances?" Christianity is nothing less than *all of Him* in *all of you!*

To understand the reality of His indwelling, we need to understand three things: 1) the reality of *Who*

He is; 2) the reality of *Where He is;* 3) the reality of *Why He is, Who He is, Where He is.*

THE REALITY OF WHO HE IS

Who exactly is the Christ received by sinners to indwell their lives? Jesus answered this Himself when He said, "Before Abraham was I am," (John 8:58). In making this statement, Christ took upon Himself the title by which God described Himself to Moses in Exodus 3:14. The Jews who heard this claim recognized the significance of Christ's claim to deity, and promptly took up stones to stone Him. The significance of the claim in the present context is that Christ is the great I AM — the unchanging One. It was impossible for Christ to have said, "Before Abraham was, I was," or "After you die, I will be," because He is the One who inhabits eternity and therefore strictly He cannot say, "I am," "I was," "I will be," but simply, continually, "I am." Therefore, all that Jesus Christ ever was, *He is,* and all that He ever will be, *He is.* In a previous chapter, we looked at the fullness of His life as a historical fact, but now we must recognize that all that He was in the historical past, *He is* today. The thought of the glorified, triumphant Christ in the future often fills our hearts with hope and anticipation, but it is always thrilling to remember that all that He will be *He is* today. "Jesus Christ, the same yesterday, today, and for ever" (Hebrews 13:8) is today all that He ever was and all that He ever will be: and all that He is, *He is* in us.

If you get excited about the Christ who fed the 5,000, you should be constantly and equally excited about the Christ who lives within you, because He is exactly the same Christ! All that He ever was, *He is.* His glorious magnificence demonstrated in the feeding of the 5,000 is the identical, glorious magnificence wherewith He is filled as He lives within you.

We have seen that the fullness of Christ was a direct result of His dependence upon, and obedience to, the Father whose He was, and whom He served. Now, let us look a little deeper into His inner relationship so that we may more fully appreciate the reality of who He is. "For it has pleased the Father that all the divine fullness — the sum total of the divine perfection, powers, and attributes — should dwell in Him permanently" (Colossians 1:19, Amplified New Testament); "For in Him the whole fullness of Deity (the Godhead) continues to dwell in bodily form — giving complete expression of the divine nature" (Colossians 2:9, Amplified New Testament). The fullness of Christ was the result of the inner "fullness of the Deity" dwelling within Him in bodily form. Finite brains can never fully understand what is meant by the "fullness of the Godhead," but we can appreciate in a small way something of what it signifies.

The Godhead consists of the Father, Son and Holy Spirit, and the attributes of all three, the divine Trinity, chose to take up permanent residence in Christ, and were delighted to use Him as a means of finite expression. The numerous titles God used in Scripture variously describe His divine attributes, and it was these attributes that found their full expression in Christ, for in Him dwelt "the sum total of the divine perfections, powers, and attributes." God is the "God of patience" (Romans 15:5); "the God of peace" (Romans 15:33); the "God of love" (II Corinthians 13:11); the "God of eternal power" (Romans 1:20); the God of "all comfort" (II Corinthians 1:3), etc., and therefore His divine attributes are patience, peace, love, eternal power, all comfort, and many more. Jesus Christ, in whom all these attributes dwelt in fullest measure, drew upon them and therefore demonstrated the patience of God, the peace of God, the love of God, the eternal power of God, and the all-prevailing comfort of God, in His earthly life. Now that He indwells the believer, His intention is to invest these same attributes in him, and demonstrate them through his earthly life. The weakest saint who has received Christ, has received the Christ in whom the eternal power of the Godhead is invested. The most ungracious, impatient servant of God has within him the Christ in whom all the fullness of the Godhead dwells, including all the grace, and lovingkindness of God. This must be appreciated in these days, because it is patently obvious that many saints regard their weaknesses and shortcomings as something that they must live with and they fail to recognize that the Christ who lives within them is the complete antithesis of all weakness and sin. Weakness can become a habit, and can be regarded as inevitable normality, but this idea must be abandoned when it is fully grasped who Christ is as He lives within the Christian.

It is not surprising that Paul could not wait beyond the third verse of his Ephesian Epistle before bursting into — "Blessed be the God and Father of our Lord Jesus Christ who hath blessed us with all spiritual blessings in heavenly places in Christ (Ephesians 1:3), because he had discovered that all spiritual blessings were simply the attributes of God's Person, and all these attributes had their permanent abode in Christ, and Christ was in him. This glorious realization filled and flooded his life. Evidently the Ephesians had not seen the wonder of the indwelling Christ because Paul's prayer was, "The eyes of your heart flooded with light so that you can know and understand the hope to which

He has called you and *how rich is His glorious inheritance in the saints* — His set apart ones" (Ephesians 1:8, Amplified New Testament). Therefore we can see that in Christ dwells all the fullness of God; Christ is in us, therefore in us all the fullness of God is made real in the Person of Christ.

In us are invested all the divine qualities of love, peace, power, and patience because all that Christ ever was, He is, and all that He is, He is in us. This is the shattering reality of who He is, as He indwells us.

THE REALITY OF WHERE HE IS

Music in the mind of Mozart brought no pleasure to anyone, and a beautiful scene in the imagination of Michelangelo stirred no emotions because the hidden capabilities and attributes of both masters required a medium of expression. Mozart required musicians, instruments and score, and Michelangelo was helpless without canvas, brushes and paint, but given the right material, both men were able to express their genius. God has chosen man as the instrument whereby His attributes might be expressed and demonstrated to the praise of His own glory, the blessing of the world, and the untold joy and fulfillment of the man acting as the instrument. It is in a human being that the living Christ in all the fullness of the Godhead dwells and works. Much is said about Christ walking alongside, going ahead, and overshadowing, but the main thrust of New Testament teaching is undoubtedly that Christ is *within*.

The passage quoted above from Ephesians chapter three, speaks of the personality, the heart, the inner man, and the body as being the centers in which Christ lives, and the areas in which He works.

Christ Indwelling the Heart. The Bible definition of the heart differs from the physiological definition. In Scripture, the heart is regarded as the center of intellectual, emotional, and volitional activity, while a layman (such as myself), completely bereft of physiological terminology, would define the heart simply as a blood-pump! The Jews had hard hearts (this means their wills — Mark 3:6), the scribes had reasoning hearts (this means their intellects — Mark 2:8), and the disciples of Emmaus had burning hearts (this means their emotions — Luke 24:32). Thus it can be seen that Scripture regards the heart as the center of the will, intellect and emotion.

When the Christ, in whom all the fullness of the Godhead dwells, indwells the emotions of a redeemed sinner, He is capable of reproducing heavenly love. Christ in the believer's will can produce heavenly decisions and heavenly priorities, and His activity in the intellect can result in heavenly wisdom. Heavenly love, heavenly wisdom, heavenly priorities and heavenly choices are the spiritual fruits of Christ indwelling the heart.

Christ Indwelling the Personality. It is interesting to note that the Lord made men with the basic personality necessary for the task for which He had created them. It was never necessary for Him to change the basic structure of a man's personality, but He always found it necessary to channel it afresh, and of course, He still does find it necessary. Saul of Tarsus, the brilliant Jew, became Paul the Apostle, the brilliant epistle-writer; Saul, the implacable opponent of Christianity, became Paul, the irrepressible servant of Christ; Saul, the "exceedingly mad" persecutor, became Paul, the fool for Christ's sake. The reckless, brilliant, intense, outstanding Saul, driven by Satan, became the reckless, brilliant, intense, outstanding Paul, indwelt by Christ. A man's personality is basically ideal for the purpose for which God made it, and only needs the indwelling Saviour's dynamic to channel it properly, and use it to the full.

Christ Indwelling the Inner Man. "Though our outer man is (progressively) decaying and wasting away, yet our inner self is being (progressively) renewed day after day" (II Corinthians 4:16, Amplified New Testament). In this verse, Paul drew a distinction between his body, which was progressively disintegrating (and that was not surprising!), and his inner man, which was progressively being renewed and refreshed. Obviously the inner man, in contradistinction to the outer man, must be the part of man made by God, exclusively for Himself, where man can enjoy God, and God can enjoy man. This is the place of hidden communion and vital relationship deep down in the hidden recesses of a man's being. It is in the inner man that a human being has the capability of worshiping and knowing his God.

The Lord said that worship was a spiritual exercise, and must be carried out "in spirit and in truth (reality)" (John 4:24, Amplified New Testament). The reality of worship is utterly dependent upon the activity of Christ in the inner man, as He stimulates to overflowing praise and adoration. It is perfectly true that beautiful music, fine buildings, gorgeous flowers, and flowing words can be a tremendous help in worship, but all these things must be regarded as purely secondary to Christ. Probably some of the most glorious worship services ever held took place in the Catacombs of Rome, and it is doubtful whether the music, buildings, flowers or words were of the highest order in that particular environment. Worship which is dependent upon external embellishments to the exclusion of the activity of Christ in the inner man is worship which has degenerated into a mechanical performance, and even the most polished performance can only parody the spiritual exercise which is the reality of worship. There is no substitute in worship for the working of the indwelling Christ in the inner man.

CHRIST INDWELLING THE BODY

The indwelling of Christ is essentially practical, because He indwells the body — that part of man which walks and talks, touches and sees, rises and sleeps. His intention in indwelling the body is to *control* its *use*, and to *condemn* its *abuse*. No child of God, fully appreciating the wonder of His presence within, will desire to abuse his body with immoral, wasteful, harmful, extravagant activities.

On the other hand, it is man's body which can become an instrument whereby Christ moves, speaks, sees and works in the twentieth century. "I appeal to you therefore, brethren, and beg of you in view of (all) the mercies of God, to make a *decisive dedication of your bodies* — presenting all your members and faculties — as a living sacrifice, holy (devoted, consecrated) and well pleasing to God, which is your reasonable (rational, intelligent) service and spiritual worship" (Romans 12:1, Amplified New Testament).

A donkey's body proved to be an ideal platform for Christ on the original Palm Sunday, and because the donkey was the vehicle of His movement, He was recognized and glorified, and there is no limit to the usefulness of a Christ-indwelt human body. When the various faculties and members of the body are abandoned to the dynamic of the indwelling Christ, the body arrives at its true fulfillment.

Where Christ *is* in reality is of great significance to the believer, because as the Christ of Godhead fullness, His life in a personality and heart can have great *social* impact. His mastery of a body will bring untold *physical* benefit, and the inner man filled with the fullness of Christ, will enjoy heaven day by day, even when surrounded by the mundane, harrassing pressures of modern life, and this is the reality of *spiritual* experience.

THE REALITY OF WHY HE IS, WHO HE IS, WHERE HE IS

Jesus Christ, the great I AM is the One in whom all the fullness of the Godhead dwells — this is "the reality of who He is"; He lives in you — this is "the reality of where He is." Anyone grasping the significance of this will obviously be most anxious to have an intelligent comprehension of the reason. If God decreed that Christ should indwell a believer, obviously He had an intelligent reason for making the decree; and if Christ "in whom are hid all the treasures of wisdom and knowledge" (Colossians 2:3) deigned to take up residence within the humblest believer's heart, presumably He knew why.

It is also quite reasonable to assume that if God was so concerned that men should recognize the indwelling presence of Christ, He would take the trouble to outline the purpose of this glorious indwelling. God wants every Christian to know *why He is*, who He is, and where He is! Paul said, "I have been crucified with Christ — (in Him) I have shared His crucifixion; it is no longer I who live, but *Christ, the Messiah, lives in me;* and the life I now live in the body I live by faith — by adherence to and reliance on and (complete) trust — in the Son of God, Who loved me and gave Himself up for me" (Galatians 2:20, Amplified New Testament).

"But if *Christ lives in you,* (then although your natural) body is dead by reason of sin and guilt, the spirit is alive because of (the) righteousness (that He imputes to you)" (Romans 8:10, Amplified New Testament). "When *Christ Who is our life* appears, then you also will appear with Him in (the splendor of His) glory" (Colossians 3:4, Amplified New Testament).

It is not necessary to look in Scripture long or hard to discover the reason why Christ indwells a Christian. When Christ came to live in you, He simply came to *live.* On a number of occasions I have asked Christians the question, "When Jesus Christ came to live in you, what did He come to do?" Often I have been amazed at the mystified, irrelevant answers given. The answer is so vital, and yet so simple. When Jesus Christ came to live in you, Jesus Christ came *to live in you.* He did not come into your life to be a *passive nonentity;* He came to be an *active reality.*

Life is a vibrant, vital experience — if it ceases to be either vital or vibrant, it ceases to be life, and when Christ came into your heart, He came to be your life — a vital, vibrant experience to be reckoned with, and a power to be relied upon.

It is difficult to define life, but I suppose a simple definition could be "the state of being." Jesus Christ, the Eternal I Aм, came to live in you, in other words to take up a state of being in your humanity. If Jesus Christ is *to be,* He can only *be Himself,* and when Jesus Christ is given the right to be Himself in you, then "the sky is the limit." The fullness of Christ is the outcome of Jesus Christ being Himself in you, and His sole purpose in coming into you was to *be Himself.* Think for just a moment; allow your mind to traverse the vista of truth this reveals; give your imagination the right to roam the untold possibilities! Jesus Christ *living* (being Himself) — all that He ever was, and will be — *in you*. This is the reality of *why He is* who He is, where He is.

Not only is it a tremendous privilege to recognize the significance of the above, but the value is multiplied a thousandfold when you understand that His indwelling is more than a tremendous privilege; it is a vital necessity. You may have noticed in the quotations given above, that in Galatians 2:20, "Christ lives in me" was coupled with the statement, "I have been crucified." In Romans 8:10, "Christ lives in you" was linked with "the body is dead." Colossians 3:4 says, "Christ is our life" as an amplification of Colossians 3:3 which says "you have died." On each occasion, Scripture stresses that the life of Christ is the antithesis of the deadness of man.

When Christ came to live in you, He came to be Himself — that is wonderful — but this is not only delightful, theological truth — it is a matter of life and death, for He came to impart His life in the area of your death. "I have been crucified . . . *but* Christ lives in me." "You are dead . . . *but* Christ is our life." "Christ lives in you . . . although your body is dead . . . the spirit is alive." Christ came to live in you in all the fullness of the Godhead to take the place of your deadness. His indwelling is the only answer to what you are — dead. If Jesus Christ living within you is the only answer to what God says you are — dead — it is obvious that unless Christ is allowed to be Himself in the place of what you are, you are bound to dismal failure.

Failure to enjoy life is always sad, but in the spiritual realm, failure to appropriate the life of Christ in the area of death is stark tragedy. Because the life of

Christ within a Christan (God's only answer to man's deadness) is not fully understood and enjoyed, there is much evangelical inactivity, sterility and carnality today.

It is quite common to meet a Christian who recognizes his weakness and says, "Amen" to the doctrine that He is "dead" and "crucified with Christ" — and yet fails to appropriate Christ as his life. Christ does not intend to bolster up our deadness or to encourage our weakness; He is not concerned to help us to be what we are not, or to urge us to do what we cannot. He came to be life in our deadness, to demonstrate Himself as the Resurrection and the Life in the area of our total inability.

When Jesus stood at the grave of Lazarus, He did not encourage Lazarus and He did not urge him; He did not teach him, and He did not give him a glorious example. All He did was to *be Himself*, and thus He proved in Lazarus, who was totally dead, that He is "the Resurrection and the Life." He superseded the deadness of Lazarus with the life of Himself, and that is all He came to do for you — to be Himself in exchange for what you are. "For you are coming progressively to be acquainted with and to recognize more strongly and clearly the grace of our Lord Jesus Christ —His kindness, His gracious generosity, His undeserved favor and spiritual blessing; (in) that though He was (so very) rich, yet for your sakes He became (so very) poor, in order that by His poverty you might become enriched — abundantly supplied" (II Corinthians 8:9, Amplified New Testament). Christ the rich, became Christ the poor, that you, the poor, might become you, the rich. Christ exchanged His riches for your poverty that you might exchange your poverty for His riches. His glorious offer was that you should trade your deadness for His life. Have you accepted the offer?

6

The Divine Presence

PRIVILEGES AND RESPONSIBILITIES ARE LIKE TWINS — THEY always come in pairs! The privilege of being blessed is invariably linked with the responsibility of being a blessing. We have already seen this was true in Abraham's life, and the Lord underlined the principle in John 7:37, 38, "In the last day, that great day of the feast, Jesus stood and cried, saying, If any man thirst, let him come unto me, and drink. He that believeth on me, as the scripture hath said, out of his belly shall flow rivers of living water." He promised refreshing, life-giving water to the thirsty soul of any man, and the reception of this life-giving water is a glorious privilege. Then He pointed out that the refreshed recipient of blessing was to become automatically the channel of identical blessing to others — responsibility. The infilling water which satisfies the thirst is to become the out-flowing water which meets the needs of others.

When God gave you the gift of reconciliation with one hand, He also gave you the Gospel of reconciliation with the other. To *experience* reconciliation is your privilege, but to *expound* reconciliation is your responsibility. "And all things are of God, who *has reconciled us* to Himself by Jesus Christ, and *has given to us* the ministry of reconciliation" (II Corinthians 5:18). Perhaps in some hour of deep distress you have experienced the comfort of God, and you rejoiced in the privilege of being comforted by the God of all comfort. However, you were not comforted solely to weather your hour of deep distress, but to be in a position to comfort others with the self-same God-given comfort. "Who comforteth us in all our tribulation, that we may be able to comfort them which are in any trouble, by the comfort wherewith we ourselves are comforted of God" (II Corinthians 1:4). From these examples it will be seen that privileges and responsibilities are heavenly twins.

The highest privilege that was ever granted to you was that the Risen Christ in all His fullness should take up residence in your heart and come to live within you. Naturally, such an enormous privilege carries a corresponding responsibility.

THE RESPONSIBILITY OF HIS INDWELLING

Imagine for a moment that I accept the privilege of entertaining an honored guest in my home When he arrives at the front door, I welcome him and ask him to step inside. He has traveled for many hours, but I do not invite him to sit down. He has not eaten for some considerable time, but I offer him no food or refreshment. He is obviously extremely tired, but no bedroom is available to him, and because his shoes are travel-stained, I ask him to remove them in case he should soil the carpet; but I constantly assure him how privileged I consider myself to be, that such an honored guest should come to stay in my home!

Obviously he would not believe me, because he would know that when I accepted the privilege of welcoming him, I automatically accepted the responsibility of making him feel at home. Social manners demand that every guest should be allowed to settle down and feel at home, and failure to insure that this takes place is failure in responsibility and abuse of privilege.

I think in this case the honored guest would pack his honored bags, and beat a hasty retreat!

Social etiquette is one thing, but Scriptural exhortation is another: "May Christ through your faith (actually) dwell — settle down, abide, make His permanent home — in your hearts" (Ephesians 3:17, Amplified New Testament). Many Christians fail to differentiate between Christ *living* in them, and Christ *dwelling* in them. In II Corinthians 13:5 Paul defined a Christian as being a person in whom Christ lives, but as we have just seen in Ephesians 3:17, he prayed that the Christians might allow Christ to dwell in them. If living and dwelling are synonymous, then Paul was contradicting himself and praying for something that had already happened according to his own definition. However, to dwell means "to settle down and to feel at home," and while the Christian's privilege is to have Christ living within, his responsibility is to make absolutely certain that Christ is allowed to settle down and feel at home!

Please note carefully that Christ is made to feel at home "through your faith." Your responsibility is to make the honored guest feel at home, and your sole means of doing this is faith. Feeling at home is not a crisis, but a process, and therefore if Christ is to continually feel at home in a believer's heart, it must be as a result of a continual attitude of faith on the part of the believer. Four times in Scripture we read, "The just shall live by faith," and I am quite certain that this principle is of prime importance, or Scripture would not repeat it four times. Also, we read, "But without faith it is impossible to please and be satisfactory to Him" (Hebrews 11:6, Amplified New Testament). The one principle upon which the Christian life operates is the principle of faith. It is by faith and faith alone in the Person of the indwelling Lord Jesus that He is made to feel at home and allowed to be Himself.

When you became a child of God, you did so by grace through faith. "For by grace are ye saved through faith; and that not of yourselves: it is the gift of God" (Ephesians 2:8). Grace was God's part, and faith was your part, and when you had made that *initial act* of faith which allowed Christ to come to live in you, you did not then exhaust all need for faith. The *initial act* of faith which allows Christ to enter and live within the heart, must be extended into a *continual attitude* of faith in His Person which allows Him to settle down and feel at home.

It is amazing how many of God's people decide that once they have received Christ by faith, they no longer need to exercise faith. But it must be understood that faith in the living, indwelling Christ within is as vital to daily life as faith in the dying Christ on the Cross is indispensable for salvation, and faith in the glorified, enthroned Christ is necessary for eternal security. When you can cease to trust the Christ who died for you for forgiveness of sins, you can immediately cease trusting the Christ who lives within you as your daily life. Immediately you come to the conclusion that you need no longer trust the Christ who is glorified and enthroned, for your eternal security, you will be perfectly in order to dispense with an attitude of faith in the living, risen, indwelling Christ whom you have invited to live within you. No sane, Bible-taught Christian would contemplate the possibility of forgiveness of sins apart from faith in a crucified Christ, or one's eternal security apart from faith in the glorified Christ, and therefore every sane, Bible-taught Christian has no logical alternative to a life of faith in the indwelling Christ.

Your faith must be a constant attitude of dependence upon Him: a continual appropriating of all the riches that you have in Him, and a step-by-step expectation in Him to be Himself within you. This is faith, and this is your responsibility, but of course it is possible to accept the privilege and abuse the responsibility: to have Him *live* within you, and yet not *dwell* within you.

We can illustrate this from the story found in Mark 4:35-41. One day the disciples invited the Lord Jesus to come into their boat. He was given a cordial welcome and ushered to the back of the boat, and then left alone. The master of the ship took control and headed out into the open water. Subsequently, a storm arose and the boat, with the living Christ on board, began to sink. There was not the slightest doubt as to who He was, and there was no doubt at all as to where He was. He was occupying a seat in the stern, and He was fast asleep. It seems fantastic that a boat containing the living Christ should be in danger of sinking, but we know how possible it is for a life containing the living Christ to founder and sink, because He occupies the back seat and has been disregarded and neglected for so long that it appears He has gone to sleep.

Jesus Christ did not come on board to occupy the back seat, but to be Himself. He was not interested in sleeping, but in living. The horrible truth was that He was forgotten and discounted — unnecessary "cargo" on board a sinking ship, and most definitely not "at home." Eventually, when the storm became too much for the master of the ship, he remembered who Christ was, and where He was, and ran to Him, awoke Him, and blamed Him for all that had gone wrong. The Lord Jesus did not answer the unwarranted criticism, but stood up, rebuked the wind, and immediately there was a great calm. He was simply Himself in this situation, and the result was that He demonstrated His glory in their battered, sinking ship. The storm promptly admitted defeat and fled behind the Galilean hills, and a great and wonderful peace prevailed. The Lord Jesus calmly turned to them and said, "How is it that you have no faith?" (Mark 4:40).

Without faith it is impossible to please Him, and it is through faith that we make Him settle down and feel at home. Not for one moment had they drawn upon His divine resources or thrilled to His divine presence. They had welcomed Him on board, and promptly forgotten Him, and the result was that they had failed lamentably in their responsibility of allowing Him, through their faith, to settle down and feel at home. They had treated Him as a *passenger* rather than *pilot*, and regarded Him as *cargo* rather than *captain*. Has the initial act of faith which allowed Christ to enter into your heart and life become a continual attitude of faith which allows Him to be Himself in you? Is He passenger or pilot, captain or cargo?

When I was a little boy, I once heard an old coal-miner relate a simple but moving story. He told about being summoned to Buckingham Palace by the late King George V to be decorated for extreme bravery in a coal-mine explosion. He described the magnificent investiture-room, and said that he just longed to escape, for he felt completely out of place in such luxurious surroundings. However, there was one young man in the palace who seemed completely at home; he was the King's son. The old miner said he could not wait to get back to his little white-washed cottage, and the King's son was quite happy to remain in the palace. One was only at home in a humble cottage, and the other in a glorious palace, simply because they were born and had lived all their lives in totally different strata of society. Pigs adore a muddy sty; eagles invariably nest on craggy heights. You could never make a pig settle down on a craggy height or an eagle in a muddy sty, because they are totally different in every respect; they belong to different strata of animal society.

Did you ever study the stratum of society to which the Lord Jesus belongs? Have you ever, since the day you received Him, carefully searched your heart and life to discover if it is suitable for His presence and purpose? Perhaps you have never really discovered the majesty of His person and the immensity of His purpose? Let us look into these things a little more thoroughly, in order to ascertain if He is at home in our lives.

Paul called the Lord by His title of "Christ" when he prayed, "May *Christ* dwell in your hearts . . ." The word, "Christ," is a title meaning "The Anointed One." The Old Testament speaks of three classes of people who were anointed — prophets, priests and kings. Elisha was anointed prophet (I Kings 19:16); Aaron was anointed priest (Leviticus 8:12); and David was anointed king (I Samuel 16:13). Christ, God's Anointed One, is God's Prophet — the link between God and man whereby God speaks and reveals Himself to man; He is God's Priest — the link between man and God whereby man, estranged from God can be reconciled to God, and be restored to contact with God; He is the King of Kings, and He "shall reign for ever and ever."

Moses, the prophet, was given a glorious epitaph in Scripture, ". . . and there rose not a prophet since in Israel like unto Moses, whom the Lord knew face to face" (Deuteronomy 34:10). This greatest and most glorious of prophets however was eclipsed by Christ, God's Prophet — "For this man was counted worthy of *more glory than Moses,* inasmuch as He who has builded the house has more honour than the house" (Hebrews 3:3). The office of High Priest was one of dignity and honor, and Aaron was ordained by God to fulfill this high calling: "And no man taketh this honour unto himself, but he that is *called of God, as was Aaron*" (Hebrews 5:4), but the Lord Jesus Christ surpassed all the honor, glory and dignity of the High Priestly calling of Aaron, for as God's High Priest we read, ". . . Jesus has become the Guarantee of a better (stronger) agreement — a more excellent and more advantageous covenant" (Hebrews 7:22, Amplified New Testament).

Solomon the king was outstanding as an administrator, architect and author, and he earned international repute. "And Solomon's wisdom excelled the wisdom of all the children of the east country, and all the wisdom of Egypt, for he was wiser than all men . . . and his fame was in all nations round about" (I Kings 4:30, 31). The skeptical Queen of Sheba, when she saw all the magnificence of the glorious king, was so taken aback that "there was no more spirit in her" (I Kings 10:5), yet we read of the Lord Jesus, "Behold, *a greater than Solomon* is here."

Take the greatest prophet, the most gracious priest and the most glorious king, add all their attributes, and their sum total will amount to no more than a fraction of the greatness, glory and grace of God's Prophet, Priest and King — the Christ. He it is whom you have received as your honored guest. He is higher than the highest, mightier than the mightiest, lovelier than the loveliest and He is *in you!* Has He found an ideal home in the inner recesses of your life?

AN IDEAL HOME FOR A PROPHET

"And it fell on a day, that Elisha passed to Shunem, where was a great woman; and she constrained him to eat bread. And so it was, that as oft as he passed by, he turned in thither to eat bread. And she said unto her husband, Behold, now, I perceive that this is an holy man of God, which passeth by us continually. Let us make a little chamber, I pray thee, on the wall; and let us set for him there a bed, and a table, and a stool, and a candlestick: and it shall be, when he cometh to us, that he shall turn in thither" (II Kings 4:8-10). Here we have a description of an ideal residence for a prophet. It is important to note that this residence was ideal because it was built by a woman who desired to make the best facilities available, and she was in a position to do so. She was a "great" woman, and this word "great" refers to her wealth and not her weight, her substance and not her circumference! She had all the resources necessary to build an ideal residence, and build it she did.

It was no palace, but it was ideal even though it consisted solely of one room, and four articles of furniture. This does not sound too exciting, and I do not suppose any of us would have left our own homes to live in it, but I am sure that Elisha loved his little home and really settled down there. There was nothing ostentatious about the residence, because the accent was on usefulness. As far as Elisha was concerned, every department of his residence was to be immediately useful, and continually available, because he had no time to waste on secondary matters. This, of course, is the ideal home for a prophet, usefulness and availability dictating the decor.

You invited the Prophet who is greater than the greatest to live in your heart, and your responsibility is to give Him an ideal residence and allow Him to feel at home there. Jesus Christ is in business in real earnest, and He is concerned that His residence should be stripped for action, and that all extraneous, ostentatious affairs of the heart should be cleared in order that He Himself may go on unhindered in His divine activity. Remember that it is possible for "encumbrance — unnecessary weight" (Hebrews 12:1, Amplified New Testament) to fill a life and, of course, when this occurs the Prophet is limited in His work. Encumbrances and weights need not necessarily be sins, but they must be dealt with if the ideal residence is to be made available for the greatest Prophet of all. Therefore, to fulfill your responsibility, it is imperative that you allow Him to examine carefully the furniture of your life and show you what is getting in His way, and then to be prepared to lay aside anything, or anybody, who He decides is a weight or a hindrance — an unnecessary embellishment in a life that is designed to be practically effective as the residence of God's Prophet on earth.

An Ideal Home for a Priest

It was in the Temple that the priest engaged in his service, and here he knew that he was the man of God's choice in the place of God's choice, representing the people of God's choice in the method of God's choice. Under these circumstances he could not fail to "feel at home." Aaron, the great High Priest had his limitations (he died, for instance!), but Jesus Christ is greater than Aaron for we read that the Father said of Him, "You are a *priest* for ever" (Hebrews 7:21, Amplified New Testament).

The place of Aaron's priestly activity was designed in detail by God and therefore it must have been ideal.

The Priest who surpasses Aaron has chosen human
hearts to be His sphere of activity, and in the believer's
heart he needs an ideal sanctuary. The individual believer is reminded, "Do you not know that your body is
the *temple—the very sanctuary—*of the Holy Spirit Who
lives within you, Whom you have received (as a gift)
from God?" (I Corinthians 6:19, Amplified New Testament), and the corporate body of Christ, His Church,
needs constantly to remember, "In Him — and in fellowship with one another — you yourselves also are
being built up (into this structure) with the rest, to
form a fixed abode (dwelling place) of God in (by,
through) the Spirit" (Ephesians 2:22, Amplified New
Testament).

When the Lord entered the temple in Jerusalem,
He looked round the court of the Gentiles and saw all
sorts of shady transactions taking place as money was
changed, and beasts were sold for sacrifices. He calmly
and deliberately made a whip of cords and proceeded
to drive out men, cattle, sheep and pigeons; He over-
threw tables full of coins and rapidly cleared the temple
of all that was going on inside its precincts. He was
no "gentle Jesus meek and mild" on this occasion, but
rather a man burning with zeal, full of the courage of
His convictions, and utterly fearless of the consequences
of His drastic actions. The reason was that as a Priest
coming into His temple, He did not feel at home —
in fact He felt strongly about the abuse of the "habitation of God," and He emphasized His point with the
aid of a whip.

What was it that stirred the great High Priest to
such violent action? The Jews were intended to sacrifice animals in the temple, and the tribute had to be
paid, therefore it was extremely convenient for the
worshipers to change the foreign currency on the

premises, and to be able to buy the animals for sacrifice in the court of the Gentiles instead of driving them many miles from home. It was *convenience* that dominated the thoughts of the worshipers as they made their way to the temple, and the fact that the temple had been set apart to be pure and holy and utterly separate from anything that might savor of shady practice was unimportant to them.

"In that day shall there be upon the bells of the horses, HOLINESS UNTO THE LORD; and the pots in the Lord's house shall be like the bowls before the altar. Yea, every pot in Jerusalem and in Judah shall be holiness unto the Lord of hosts: and all they that sacrifice shall come and take of them, and seethe therein: and in that day there shall be no more the Canaanite in the house of the Lord of hosts" (Zechariah 14:20, 21). The Lord takes His temple seriously, and even the bells of the horses, and the pots and bowls, should be distinctively holy. There is no place for the Canaanite in the house of the Lord of hosts, for holiness, separation and distinction are the words used to describe the ideal temple, but these things had been sacrificed for convenient, comfortable compromise in the Lord's day. Christ was not objecting to cattle in the court, but to compromise in the heart.

"(Come) and as living stones be yourselves built (into) a spiritual house, for a holy (dedicated, consecrated) priesthood, to offer up (those) *spiritual sacrifices* (that are) acceptable and well-pleasing to God through Jesus Christ" (I Peter 2:5, Amplified New Testament). Jesus Christ, the Great High Priest in your heart, His temple, expects you to offer up spiritual sacrifices, and the word "sacrifice" means exactly what it says — sacrifice. The temple that knows no sacrifice but only compromise is the temple where the great

High Priest must invariably be grieved and limited. David said, "Neither will I offer burnt offerings to the Lord my God of that which *costs me nothing*" (II Samuel 24:24).

Jesus loves the heart utterly available to Him, and He grieves over the heart totally closed to Him, and the heart that specializes in compromise to the exclusion of the other two possibilities is the heart in which He can never under any circumstances feel at home. Speaking to the Laodicean Church, He said, "Would that you were either cold or hot! So, because you are lukewarm, and neither cold nor hot, I will spue you out of my mouth!" (Revelation 3:15, 16, Amplified New Testament). If you run away from any Christian experience, service or activity which entails a costly spiritual sacrifice and promply seek refuge in compromise, be absolutely certain that your life is not the Great High Priest's idea of an ideal temple. Your responsibility is to make Him feel at home, and this He can never be if you prefer convenient, comfortable compromise to all-out abandoned availability.

An Ideal Home for a King

The temple which Solomon built was magnificent. Even in the twentieth century, Solomon's temple is a by-word, and it is certain that no efforts were spared in making a first-class job of the residence for the most high God. David had longed to build the Lord a house because he was embarrassed that he should live in a house of cedar wood, and yet the Ark of the Lord should be deposited in a tent. The honor of building such a house was not granted to David, but Solomon, his son, was given the task and with all his considerable abilities and means he set to work. After much labor and activity the great day came when Solomon dedicated the completed house to the service of the Lord. This was the culmination of seven years of hard work.

It seems odd that having spent *seven* years building a house for the Lord, Solomon found it necessary to spend *thirteen* years building his own house! If the temple was magnificent, presumably the private residence which took almost twice as long to build must have been fit for a king! It was an ideal home for a king.

Solomon built his private residence in close proximity to the temple which we know was erected on Ornan's threshing floor. This threshing floor was in all probability an out-crop of rock on which the farmer Ornan did his work. King David bought the site from him, and built an altar upon it because God directed him so to do. "Then the angel of the Lord commanded Gad to say to David, that David should go up and set up an altar unto the Lord in the threshing-floor of Ornan the Jebusite" (I Chronicles 21:18). God in His wonderful plan chose a slab of rock to be bought with a price with a view to its becoming the habitation of a king. A slab of rock, a purchased possession, and a king's residence — this was the history of the site!

When God made you, He had every intention of taking the slab of rock which men call a heart, purchasing it for Himself by the blood of the Lord Jesus Christ, and making it into a royal residence. "A new heart also will I give you, and a new spirit will I put within you; and I will take away the *stony heart* out of your flesh, and I will give you an heart of flesh. And *I will put my Spirit within you,* and cause you to walk in my statutes, and ye shall keep my judgments, and do them" (Ezekiel 36:26, 27).

God has planned and promised to work on the coldest, hardest rock-like heart, and to remake it into a warm, pulsating, Spirit-filled residence, but of course He expects the cooperation of the believer in the form of simple, expectant and obedient faith. God worked this kind of miracle in Paul, in John and in Peter, and right through the history of the Christian Church, He has been fulfilling His promise and proving that He can build royal palaces on slabs of rock. How is His building progressing in your life? Has the King settled down in the Royal residence?

It was a Glorious House — filled with light! "And there were windows in three rows, and light was against light in three ranks" (I Kings 7:4). There were no dark corners, and no spooky cellars, but the light of God flooded the building in every part and the king loved it that way because it was his design. It says of the King of Kings and Lord of Lords in I Timothy 6: 16 (Amplified New Testament), "Who alone has immortality (in the sense of exemption from every kind of death) and lives in *unapproachable light* . . ." and the Lord Jesus was with the Father before the world was made. It was in the unapproachable light of God Himself that the Lord Jesus spent the by-gone ages of eternity. See the contrast: "Son of Man, hast thou seen what the ancients of the house of Israel *do in the dark*, every man in the *chambers of his imagery?* for they say, The Lord seeth us not; the Lord hath forsaken the earth" (Ezekiel 8:12). To change the dark cellars of the heart into the lofty lighted residence fit for His presence is the desire and design of the King. The King loves the light and hates the dark, hidden things, and your responsibility is to make Him feel at home — the King in His palace flooded with light. That means an attitude of heart which is continually prepared to say:

> Throw light into the darkened cells,
> Where passion reigns within;
> Quicken my conscience till it feels
> The loathesomeness of sin.
>
> Search all my thoughts, the secret springs,
> The motives that control
> The chambers where polluted things
> Hold empire o'er my soul.

It was a Glorious House — spacious and airy. A quick study of I Kings 7:1-11 reveals that Solomon's house had a spacious, intricate design. There were many rooms and porches, courts and special quarters for the queen, a throne room, and porticos all forming a complete ideal sovereign's residence. It is unthinkable that the king was denied access to any part of his own building, for he was master of his own home and welcome in every room.

You can echo the words of Scripture and point to your heart saying, "A greater than Solomon is *here!*" for the King has taken up residence in your heart. Many and devious are the compartments of the heart of man. Education, social activity, business, family, hobbies, sports, career, and a thousand other things all have their head office in the heart. The King deserves, desires and demands access to every room of your life, and whenever this is denied, the area locked to Him is nothing more than an empty, dusty, useless compartment in a palace designed for a King, and this is a heinous waste. The business that excludes Christ is a barren, albeit flourishing concern. The social round that finds Christ an embarrassment is a disgrace to a Christian. Sports, graciously blessed and honored with the King's presence, can be glorious, but locked off to Him are a sheer waste of time and energy. Is He at home in His residence — welcome in every room?

This lesson was pressed home to me a number of years ago. I had a music room in my heart which was locked to the King. It was my privilege to sing in a well-known choir and every Thursday night was spent joining with others in making glorious music, and I enjoyed this immensely. One day, I knew the King was telling me to resign from the choir and this I did, even though I could see no reason why I should. The very next day I was invited to commence a series of meetings in a village, and the meetings were to be held each Thursday night. Two or three weeks after the meetings started, an old lady came to know the Saviour, and two or three weeks later, she was dead! I have never regretted allowing the Saviour into the music room, and I am looking forward to singing with the old lady in the choirs of heaven one day!

It was a Glorious House — the place of righteous judgment. "Then he made a porch for *the throne* where he might judge, even the porch of judgment: and it was covered with cedar from one side of the floor to the other" (I Kings 7:7). When Solomon was told by the Lord, "Ask what I shall give thee" (I Kings 3:5), he delighted Him by replying, "Give therefore thy servant *an understanding heart to judge thy people,* that I may discern between good and bad, for who is able to judge this thy so great a people?" (I Kings 3:9). He was promptly endowed with unprecedented wisdom, and in his majestic residence he sat on the throne to mete out judgment and advice and to steer the destiny of "so great a people." There is no doubt at all that he knew what he was doing. Who sits on the throne of your heart — a stupid, arrogant, ignorant, despotic dictator called Self, who knows where he is going, and expects the King of Kings to acquiesce with his predetermined plans, or the One "in whom are hid all the treasures of wisdom and knowledge"? (Colossians 2:3).

Only God can steer the course of your life with divine discretion because *He* knows what *He* is doing. He is able to declare the end from the beginning to you. You have trusted Him to forgive and forget your past, and you expect Him to deliver you safely in heaven. Therefore, you *must* give Him the right to prove Himself to be as capable of organizing and directing in *time*, as you know and expect Him to be adequate for *eternity*. You have a throne room, which is His by right — is He at home sitting on His throne, ruling and reigning and signing the decrees? This is your responsibility to provide the King with a house fit for a King!

> Cleanse me from my sin, Lord,
> Put Thy power within, Lord,
> Take me as I am, Lord,
> And make me all Thine own.
> Keep me day by day, Lord,
> Underneath Thy sway, Lord,
> Make my heart Thy palace and
> Thy Royal throne.

7

Why Hath Satan Filled Your Heart?

ANANIAS AND SAPPHIRA WERE BLINDED BY THE EXAMPLE of Barnabas as he sold his land and laid the proceeds at the feet of the disciples. It appears that they were envious of the way in which he was so highly esteemed and jealous of the respect that he so deservedly received. They conspired together to sell their own land and give *part* of the proceeds to the work of the Lord, but they also decided to pretend that they were giving *all* that they possessed. Peter, with God-given insight, detected the fraud and with characteristic bluntness said, "Ananias, why hath Satan filled thine heart to lie to the Holy Ghost, and to keep back part of the price of the land? While it remained, was it not thine own? and after it was sold, was it not in thine own power? why hast thou conceived this thing in thine heart? thou hast not lied unto men, but unto God" (Acts 5: 3, 4). The result was that Ananias and Sapphira died, and the church was taught some vital lessons and "great fear came upon all the church and upon as many as heard these things" (Acts 5:11). The church learned, on that occasion, that it is possible for a child of God who should be growing into the measure of the stature of the fullness of Christ, to allow Satan to fill his heart.

Any study dealing with the fullness of Christ must look into the person and work of Satan, for he is engaged in an implacable battle against Christ and His purposes for His people. The devil is diametrically opposed to Christ, the Church of Christ and the fullness of Christ in the Christian. He is directly responsible for all the failings in the Church of Christ and all that is lacking in the life of the individual Christian. God works by addition and multiplication. "And the Lord *added* to the church daily such as should be saved" (Acts 2:47). "Grace and peace be *multiplied* unto you through the knowledge of God, and of Jesus our Lord" (II Peter 1:2). But the devil specializes in division and subtraction. His work is to disrupt the unity of the church of Christ and to bring division and discord into the fellowship of the Lord's people, and he is constantly at work subtracting or taking away from born-again Christians all that is their rightful inheritance in Christ, and in detracting from the merits of the Lord Jesus and His Word.

When a man finds Christ, the devil suffers a major set-back, but knowing full well that he can never regain the one that he has lost to Christ, he then makes it his personal responsibility to violently oppose the work of Christ within the saint. If he cannot get him back he will do all that he can to see that the child of God does not mature into the fullness of Christ, for he knows that he can expect trouble from the saint in whom Christ is at work in the power of His resurrection. Therefore, we must understand that the fullness of Christ is to be enjoyed, *despite* the considerable activity of the evil one and *in the teeth of* most violent opposition from him.

The devil is clever and wily, he is implacable and powerful, but he can make no claims to originality. God is a trinity and the devil copied the design in his fallen realm. The trinity of evil — the world, the flesh and the devil — is constantly at war with the Holy trinity — God the Father, God the Son and God the Holy Spirit. Before the dawn of history, the devil rebelled against God and made an unsuccessful attempt to make himself as big as God. He said, "I will be like the most High" (Isaiah 14:14), and Revelation 12:7 speaks of "war in heaven" as Michael and his angels fought against the dragon, ". . . that old serpent, called the Devil, and Satan, which deceiveth the whole world" (Revelation 12:9). God and Satan have been in bitter conflict since before the world came into being.

When Christ walked this earth, almost two thousand years ago, He was confronted by hostility and animosity from every angle, and the world made no secret of its rejection of Him. He was resisted at every step and He said to His disciples: "The world cannot hate you; but me it *hateth*, because I testify of it, that the works thereof are evil" (John 7:7). Eventually, He became such an embarrassment to the religious quarter of the devil's territory, that they took counsel together to put Him to death. The Lord Jesus Christ and the world were in constant conflict.

The hostility of the evil trinity to the Holy Trinity is carried on in the bitter conflict between the Holy Spirit and the flesh, "For the flesh lusteth against the Spirit, and the Spirit against the flesh; and these are contrary the one to the other" (Galatians 5:17). The Spirit and the flesh are bitterly opposed to each other — they have been since man sold himself to Satan and will be until man is finally in glory with the Saviour. It is of prime importance that the believer should understand this because he is living in "the world" which still hates Christ; his soul is the battlefield where the flesh and the Spirit are at war; and "day and night" Satan is seeking to slander and misrepresent him before the Father (Revelation 12:10). It is obvious, therefore, that if the devil himself has his representative within the believer, and this member of the trinity of evil is locked in bitter conflict with the Spirit of Christ with the sole objective of hindering the Spirit's Christ-glorifying ministry, this conflict must be resolved in favor of the Spirit of God before the fullness of Christ can ever be experienced. There is no fullness of Christ when the devil-inspired flesh is in the ascendancy and controlling the believer's life. As long as "this present evil world" (Galatians 1:4) grips a Christian's attention and pervades his thinking, the adversary will be reproducing more of his likeness than Christ will be producing His own fullness. Satan must be resisted and the victory over him must be gained constantly if the man of God is to negate the evil doings of the devil and submit to the transforming activities of the indwelling Christ. The fullness of Christ is resisted from every conceivable angle by the devil's trinity and therefore this fullness will only be experienced in the measure in which the Christian enjoys *victory* over these formidable opponents.

We have already seen that the death of Christ was the *prelude* to all Christian experience, and His life is the *pattern* of Christian experience. To be "in Christ" is the *province* of Christian experience and to have Christ in you is to possess the *power* of all Christian experience. The devil has copied these principles and perverted them for his own purposes. The principle of sinful experience can be summarized as follows:

Satan Fell —

> The *Prelude* to all sinful experience.

Satan Lives —

> The *Pattern* of all sinful experience.

The World —

> The *Province* of all sinful experience.

The Flesh —
> The *Power* of all sinful experience.

Paul was confident that the Corinthians were well versed in these facts, for speaking of the devil he said, "For we are not ignorant of his devices" (II Corinthians 2:11). But it is a fact that there are many today who are not so well informed on this subject, and consequently they are constantly defeated by the devil, drawn by the world and defiled by the flesh, with the result that the fullness of Christ is not their joyful experience. Therefore, let us discover what Scripture teaches concerning the trinity of evil.

SATAN FELL —
THE PRELUDE TO ALL SINFUL EXPERIENCE

God is perfect, and all His workmanship is perfect. Man is God's workmanship and the world is God's workmanship, but neither is perfect. This apparent contradiction is accounted for by the fact that God's man and God's world have been defiled by a power of evil and sin, not created by God. If God did not make evil and sin, and yet He made all things, then a further difficulty arises. God never made an atom bomb, but He did make an atom! He created the basic material, which was subsequently perverted to form an instrument of destruction. In the same way, He did not make sin and evil, or the devil, but He did make the basic raw materials which were perverted into sin, evil and the devil.

God made His creation capable of exercising a free will, and it is this free will, exercised anti-God, which is the root cause of all evil. The love of God requires love to satisfy it, and the heart of God yearns for the love of His creation. However, it is obvious that if God had forced man to love Him, He would have derived no satisfaction from such an emotion, for the essence of love is that it flows from a free will. It is impossible to make someone love you, and therefore it was necessary that God should equip His creation with a free will, in order that this free will might be exercised toward Him in love.

With this in mind, God made both angels and man capable of exercising their free will in His direction, and His desire was that free will should result in loving obedience and joyful dependence. God *did not make* Satan as the incarnation of evil, but He *did make* the being initially capable of loving obedience toward God, who, because he exercised his free will against God and as a result fell, became Satan, the very personification of sin and the incarnation of evil.

Jesus said, "I beheld Satan as lightning fall from heaven" (Luke 10:18), and it appears that Isaiah 14: 12-14 is an amplification of this event, although it must be admitted that it does not explicitly say so: "How art thou fallen from heaven, O Lucifer, son of the morning! how art thou cut down to the ground, which didst weaken the nations! For thou hast said in thine heart, I will ascend into heaven, I will exalt my throne above the stars of God: I will sit also upon the mount of the congregation, in the sides of the north: I will ascend above the heights of the clouds; I will be like the most High."

It can be seen that Lucifer, son of the morning, was a glorious being of great beauty, living in the presence of God and capable of free will and loving adoration. At some stage in his career, he decided in his heart that his lofty position was not lofty enough, because it was subordinate to God Himself, and he said to himself, "I will ascend . . . I will exalt . . . I will be like the most High." He was only interested in himself, and all his thinking and planning began with "I," and continued with "will." He was "I" centered, "I" controlled, and "I" interested! His God became a hindrance to his plans and an unnecessary encumbrance. He convinced himself that God was totally irrelevant to his being, for he had arrived at the conclusion that he was big enough, strong enough, and wise enough for all eventualities, and he was going to "paddle his own canoe" henceforth. Thus, the free will of God's creature was exercised against God and the initial rebellion against God took place.

All rebellion *against* God, independence *of* God, and lack of love *for* God is sin. Lucifer, son of the morning, became Satan, the origin of all sin, and he was promptly ejected from his place of high estate, and his bitter warfare against the Father had commenced. The beautiful, perfect, innocent creation of God had been tarnished by the entrance of sin, and there was war in heaven, for Satan fell. This was the grisly prelude to the awfulness of sin which has blighted the world and man ever since.

SATAN LIVES —
THE PATTERN OF ALL SINFUL EXPERIENCE

Satan began as he intended to go on. Since the day of his ejection, he has been actively antagonistic to God and all His plans and purposes. The Lord Jesus said of him, "He was a murderer from the beginning, and does not stand in the truth, because there is no truth in him. When he speaks a falsehood, he speaks what is natural to him; for he is a liar (himself) and the father of lies and of all that is false" (John 8:44, Amplified New Testament). Further, when He was speaking of the hireling who was opposed to the interest of the sheep for whom Christ died (surely this is a picture of the evil one), the Lord Jesus, in John 10:10, listed his activities as stealing, killing and destroying. Murdering, lying, stealing, destroying — this is the pattern of his life, and the pattern of all sinful experience. It flows from an attitude of rebellion against God and independence of God, and a degree of self-satisfaction and self-interest which continually says "I will," "I will," "I will." All sin is modeled upon this pattern and is utterly and totally antagonistic to God.

It is staggering to note that this pattern of sinful behavior was in evidence in the very first man who was born into the world: "And Cain talked with Abel his brother: and it came to pass, when they were in the field, that Cain rose up against Abel his brother and slew him. And the Lord said unto Cain, Where is Abel thy brother? And he said, I know not: Am I my brother's keeper?" (Genesis 4:8, 9). Cain, the world's firstborn, *murdered* his brother, and when questioned by God as to his brother's whereabouts, he *lied* — "I know not." He *robbed* his brother of life and endeavored to *destroy* his brother's simple faith in the efficacy of the burnt offering. The pattern was being well and truly followed!

Soon afterward, God examined the human race and said, "The earth is filled with violence" (Genesis 6:13). It is obvious that killing and murdering, destroying and lying were rampant in the primitive history of mankind.

David, the wonderful king, knew what it was to have sin in his life, and he conformed to the pattern, although in slightly more refined terms than Cain. He *murdered* Uriah the Hittite, without lifting a weapon more lethal than a pen dipped in ink. "And he wrote in the letter, saying, Set ye Uriah in the forefront of the hottest battle, and retire ye from him, that he may be smitten, and die" (II Samuel 11:15). He *lied* in sickly hypocrisy when he sent a message to Joab, whom he had commanded to insure that Uriah was placed in a hopeless position and he said, "Let not this thing displease thee, for the sword devoureth one as well as another" (II Samuel 11:25).

He *robbed* Uriah of his most precious possession. In fact, Nathan, the fearless prophet, described the sordid event as the stealing by a rich man of his poor neighbor's only precious little ewe lamb. David *destroyed* a home and *killed* a marriage. The pattern was plain to see. When Christ spoke to the religious Jews, who resisted him, He said, "Ye do the deeds of your father" (John 8:41), and then He added, "Ye are of your father the devil, and the lusts of your father ye will do" (John 8:44). The sin in their lives was that they set *themselves against God* (like their father), they sought to *destroy* the truth as Christ presented it, and they were ready to *kill* Him as they "took up stones to cast at him" (John 8:59).

Ananias and Sapphira sought to *rob* God, they *lied* to the Holy Spirit, knowing full well that their action, if discovered, might *destroy* the fellowship of the early church, through discord, envy and jealousy, and the result was their own *death*. In this modern age, sin still takes basically the same course and can always be attributed to the source of all evil, the devil himself, and in all sinful behavior, the pattern of his rebellion and his activity is painfully and tragically evident.

The World —
The Province of All Sinful Experience

Scripture is silent regarding the exact status of Satan before he became the Evil One, but it appears that he was an angel of great beauty and power, who wielded great authority. However, he was consistently described by the Lord Jesus as "the Prince of this World" (example: John 12:31). During the wilderness conflict with Christ, we read, "And the devil, taking him up into an high mountain, shewed unto him all the kingdoms of the world in a moment of time. And the devil said unto him, All this power will I give thee, and the glory of them: for that is delivered unto me; and to whomsoever I will I give it" (Luke 4:5,6). The Lord Jesus did not dispute the fact that the world was under the devil's control and that he had the right to administer and order it, and Scripture explicitly states, "The whole world (around us) is under the power of the evil one" (I John 5:19, Amplified New Testament).

It would appear, therefore, that as the various angels were given different responsibilities such as Israel being Michael's special charge (Daniel 12:1), Lucifer's responsibility was this world, and he maintained his control over his territory after he fell. Thus we see that the world which is God's by creation and God's by right, is under the controlling influence of the evil one and is the province of his activity. It is in this realm of satanic mastery that the child of God is born to live, and into this world he has been sent as a witness: "Go ye into all the world and preach the gospel to every creature" (Mark 16:15).

As we have already seen, the attitudes and principles of this world originated with Satan and they are basically the repudiation of God's sovereignty, and the veneration of self-sufficiency. These attitudes find expression in self-indulgence, self-gratification, self-glorification, and "self" in a thousand disguises, and invariably have their roots in a devil-inspired independence of God.

In the same way that the sphere of spiritual experience is "in Christ" and all the riches of this glorious sphere become reality through stepping out and appropriating them, so the unregenerate man spends his life appropriating the false riches of "the world," conforming to its pattern, reveling in its godless principles and living in worldly barrenness. This is a tragic condition, but there is also a grave danger for the child of God because it is possible to be "in Christ," and yet dominated by "the world."

Gross worldliness is in evidence in some Christian lives in the form of worldly appetites, activities and aspirations, and when it is understood that the world is diametrically opposed to Christ, then it will be a simple thing to see that these things can only contradict all that is of Christ in the Christian. It is not difficult to recognize gross worldliness, but there is a worldliness that is extremely subtle and equally crippling. Subtle worldliness is in evidence in an attitude of heart which repudiates the sole effectiveness of God's activity and relies upon the effectiveness of fleshly activity. It may show itself in a principle of operation which reckons only with businesslike methods and approaches and leaves no room for divine discretion and intervention. Worldly thinking and organizing of this subtle variety can put God out of business in a church today, and the devil is always delighted when his systems find an entrance into the church of Jesus Christ, rendering the presence and dynamic of the living God unnecessary and irrelevant.

The world would never run a business on the basis of a prayer meeting or in an attitude of simple dependence and expectation in an Almighty God to work His own brand of miracles. It would be considered completely unrealistic and far too heavenly minded, and of course one must agree. However, when this attitude creeps into the church, it is a manifestation of worldy thinking of satanic origin, which is utterly contradictory to the principles of divine operation. Organization is right and proper, but organization which *excludes* the *possibility* or *fails even to anticipate* the *probability* of divine intervention and godly activity is worldly thinking and cannot ever reproduce spiritual fruit. Furthermore, any "so-called" spiritual activity that is not based entirely on a simple *expectation* of the *inevitability* of Christ working in His own wonderful (and often unpredictable) way, has degenerated into a purely worldly exercise capable of achieving exactly *nothing* of spiritual consequence. God's intention is that the church should make havoc of the world, and not that the world should make havoc of the church.

The world cannot be expected to understand why a promising young man should leave his home and loved ones, sacrifice his salary and prospects, and "bury" himself in a jungle tribe. On seeing such an event, the world says, "What a waste." One would not expect the world to arrive at any other conclusion, for the world does not recognize spiritual priorities, and can see no further than materialistic benefit. We must remember that this type of thinking and method of evaluating is a product of the devil's domain, and we must recognize that materialistic worldliness has, in a number of instances, spiked the church's guns!

It is not too difficult for the world's thinking to "rub off" on saints who live much in the world, but the world's principles and programs, attitudes and activities, which invariably reckon without God, must at all costs be obliterated from the corporate life of the church, and the individual lives of the believers, for the command of God is crystal clear: "Love not the world, neither the things that are in the world" (I John 2:15). Failure to do this is to court disaster. It would be as logical to elect Karl Marx to the White House and expect him to organize a booming free enterprise system, as to invite the world to use its devilish principles to make the church a spiritual success!

THE FLESH —
THE POWER OF ALL SINFUL EXPERIENCE

The "prelude" to all sinful experience was the fall of Satan and his life is the "pattern" while the world is the "province" in which the pattern is worked out. As we saw in the principle of Christian experience, the blessings of the province ("in Christ") only become realities through the working of the power of Christian experience ("Christ in you").

The parallel is identical in the principle of sinful experience. "The flesh" in a human being is the indwelling dynamic of sin which responds to the external environment of the sinful province — the world, in the same way that the indwelling presence of Christ makes real in the believer's experience all the riches of the status of being "in Christ." It is the flesh *within* that responds to the world *without*, and the world without is dominated by Satan. As soon as a man is born again, the battle is on, for the devil is *against* him, and the world is *around* him, and the flesh is *within* him.

Many Christians fail to appreciate this, and thus are tragically disillusioned when they discover that having received Christ they are still capable of sin and failure. Remember that the devil is implacably opposed to God's purposes for you, the world around you is still antagonistic to the Christ who is your life, and the flesh within you is fighting the Spirit of God with all its considerable power. These three are your bitter enemies and they are devoted to the task of hindering the purposes and activities of the indwelling Christ by His Spirit within you in order that you might not come into "the measure of the stature of the fullness of Christ."

The devil made overtures to Ananias and Sapphira. He made various suggestions, and subtly insinuated the possibility of improving their own status and obtaining a degree of prestige which they had so far not enjoyed. They listened and were interested! The world around them had had such influence upon them that they agreed to the devilish suggestions, because they seemed to be perfectly logical. They probably thought that giving everything to the disciples was rather extreme and unbusinesslike, and yet they wanted to give the impression that they were only interested in the Lord and His work, when in fact they were interested in themselves! The devil insinuated, and the world endorsed the insinuations. However, it was the flesh within that responded to the devilish insinuations, and although the Spirit of God within them must have resisted, they allowed the flesh to take control, and they failed to allow the Spirit of God to reign in their lives. Through the indwelling presence of the flesh, Satan was allowed to "fill their hearts," and as a result dominated their wills, twisted their thinking, perverted their desires, and possessed their members.

The devil was real; the world was powerful; and the flesh within was dedicated to the task of opposition, and this trinity of evil is still as active in the twentieth century as it was in the first century!

In case you feel like running away in despair, let

me remind you of what the Bible teaches. The devil is *powerful*, but Christ came into the world, lived and died that *"He might bring to nought and make of no effect him who had the power of death, that is, the devil;* And also that He might *deliver and completely set free* all those who through the (haunting) fear of death were held in bondage throughout the whole course of their lives" (Hebrews 2:14, 15, Amplified New Testament).

The world has tremendous attraction, *but* Christ said, "I *have* overcome the world" (John 16:33). The flesh is vitally active, *but* Christ said, "Father, the hour is come. Glorify thy son that thy son also might glorify thee; *as thou hast given him power over all flesh that he should give eternal life to as many as thou hast given him.*" Rejoice in these verses, for the antagonism of the devil, the attraction of the world and the activities of the flesh *have been* countered by the living, indwelling Christ. He wants you to recognize the immensity of the opposition, so that you will glory all the more in the greatness of His victory. A little devil, a spineless world and a puny "flesh" would need little overcoming, but the evil trinity is dynamic and has been overcome by your Living Saviour. He expects you to share His victory and thereby experience His fullness in complete mastery of your considerable opponents.

8

The Man Who Followed Fully

WHAT WOULD YOU DO IF YOU MET A GIANT? TWO ALternatives spring to mind — either retreat or advance! What would you do if you met three giants? Retreat or advance? These questions are not hypothetical, but essentially practical and relevant to our study. Three giants confront every Christian — the world, the flesh, and the devil. As you are confronted with these three giants, what do you do — retreat or advance?

Caleb met three giants called Ahiman, Sheshai, and Talmai on more than one occasion. They lived in a fortified city called Hebron. The adventures of Caleb and the giants are rich in teaching for all Christians, for Caleb was a mature believer and was called by God the man who "followed me fully" (Numbers 14: 24). The Old Testament does not talk about the "fullness of Christ" for obvious reasons, but when God said that Caleb followed Him fully, He meant that Caleb lived New Testament experience in Old Testament times. Following the Lord fully entailed meeting the giants, and if the fullness of Christ is to be experienced, giants must be faced and routed.

God had planned to bring His redeemed people, Israel, out of Egypt and into Canaan. Before the children of Israel were ready to enter the land of Canaan, twelve outstanding leaders were chosen and sent by Moses to spy out the land. Caleb was one of these men, and with his eleven companions he slipped behind the enemy lines and began to explore enemy territory. As they explored, they discovered that the promises God had made to them were fully true, for the land was glorious indeed. They found a land of freshness as God had promised. "For the Lord thy God bringeth thee into a good land, a land of brooks of water, of fountains and depths that spring out of valleys and hills" (Deuteronomy 8:7). It proved to be a land of fruitfulness, ". . . a land of wheat, and barley, and vines, and fig trees and pomegranates; a land of olive oil, and honey" (Deuteronomy 8:8) and a land of fullness, ". . . A land wherein thou shalt eat bread without scarceness, thou shalt not lack anything in it; a land whose stones are iron, and out of whose hills thou mayest dig brass" (Deuteronomy 8:9).

This is a delightful picture of mature Christianity which is always characterized by freshness, fruitfulness and fullness. The fullness of Christ invariably produces a winsome, sparkling, overflowing quality of life like the brooks and wells, fountains and springs of Canaan. An abundance of fruit is inevitable when Christ is allowed to be Himself in a Christian, and there is no lack of any good thing, but rather a demonstration of utter fullness and sufficiency in the abundant sufficiency of the Living Saviour.

One day, the spies found a giant-sized bunch of grapes in the valley of Eschol, but, unfortunately, they also found a giant-sized bunch of giants! The giants spoiled their enjoyment of the grapes. You see, it is impossible to settle down to living in the land when you are going to be disturbed by a bad-tempered old giant every few minutes. You cannot eat the grapes until you have slain the giants. This is a principle of foremost importance, because no Christian can enjoy the fullness of Christ while the three giants are running wild in his life. There is no mature Christianity where the world, flesh and the devil are rampant.

Ahiman, Sheshai and Talmai were all sons of the same father — Anak. They were entirely individual in personality, but they came from a common source and appeared to be united in a common activity. Thus it can be seen that they provide a clear illustration of the giant evil trinity which confronts every Christian, for the world, the flesh and the devil are all interrelated and united in activity. As we have already seen, it is the flesh which is opposed to the operations of the indwelling Christ, and it is the flesh which works in an effort to retard and hinder the production of Christ's own fullness in the believer's life. Therefore, we will study the giant, "flesh," a little more fully.

Every Christian has ample opportunity to explore the land of freshness, fruitfulness and fullness which is God's norm of Christian experience. It is impossible for a Christian to read the Word of God and fail to see that God's brand of Christianity is superlative in the extreme. Faithful ministry of God's Word should continually face the congregation with the fullness of blessing in Christ, and Sunday by Sunday Christians should be invited to spy out the land.

The radiant life, effective service and glowing testimony of a saint who demonstrates the fullness of Christ provides opportunities to evaluate the possibilities and potential of the Christ-life, and yet it is a sordid fact that many explore the land but never enter it. Why is this? I believe it is because many Christians, having spied out the land make a report like ten of Caleb's colleagues: "And they told him, and said, We came unto the land, whither thou sentest us, and surely it floweth with milk and honey; and this is the fruit of it. Nevertheless, the people be strong that dwell in the land, and the cities are walled, and very great; and moreover we saw the children of Anak there" (Numbers 13:27, 28). The half-hearted spies made no attempt to deny the superlative qualities of the land, but having seen the giants — the children of Anak — they immediately decided to abandon the whole project of living in the land. "And there we saw the giants, the sons of Anak, which come of the giants; and we were in our own sight as grasshoppers, and so we were in their sight" (Numbers 13:33).

One look at three giants convinced ten spies of two things. First, they thought, "These giants think we are grasshoppers," and second, they thought, "When we look at these giants we are inclined to agree!" The result of the encounter was that the men of God felt like grasshoppers, and they said to themselves, "Let's get out of here," and out of Canaan they hopped, leaving three delighted giants in control of God's chosen land.

This is the experience of many today. Having tasted the possibilities, seen the potential and believed the promises of God concerning the fullness of Christ, they have been rudely reminded of the presence of the giant "flesh" and like grasshoppers have said, "Come on, let's get out of here. This kind of Christianity is unrealistic, unattainable, and unnecessary; we will settle for another kind not quite so ambitious. We will let the giants have the land and we will manage without the freshness, fruitfulness and fullness." Evangelical grasshoppers!

Praise God that Caleb "had another spirit with him" (Numbers 14:24). When he returned with his friend Joshua and the ten disillusioned, defeated spies, he repudiated their pessimistic pronouncements: "Let us go up at once and possess it, for we are well able to overcome it" (Numbers 13:30). The people were incensed by the challenging optimism of Caleb and Joshua, and tried to stone the two men who dared to believe God. However, God was delighted with the faithfulness of the two, and He said, "Doubtless ye shall not come into the land, concerning which I sware to make you dwell therein, save Caleb, the son of Jephunneh, and Joshua, the son of Nun" (Numbers 14:30). Caleb possessed the land and conquered the giants. Let us see how he achieved this remarkable feat, in order that we may apply the same principles against our giants.

CALEB RECOGNIZED THE GIANTS

Caleb was every inch a soldier. When he first saw the giants he carefully studied them, knowing full well that he must learn all that he could about the enemy. He carefully noted the giants' armor, stature and habits. Anak means "long-necked," and in all probability Anak's three giant sons had long necks like their father. Long giants have long necks. I can imagine Caleb carefully noting this as being the most vulnerable part of the giant's body. The longer the neck, the bigger the opportunity to cut the head off! Anak's long-necked sons were recognized by Caleb as immensely powerful, but equally vulnerable opponents.

He described them as "bread for us" (Numbers 14:9) — perhaps we would say that he regarded these mighty giants as "a piece of cake"! How refreshing it is to note the difference in the attitude of the ten spies and the two spies. The ten were pessimists, and the two were optimists. Someone has said that "a pessimist sees a difficulty at every opportunity, but an optimist sees an opportunity in every difficulty." Canaan, the fresh, full, fruitful land belongs to optimists. Christians have every reason to be optimistic, for the basic characteristic of their Christianity is that they possess the Risen Christ. Optimists who look at the giants and see them as glorious opportunities for the Risen Christ to vindicate Himself, and recognize their long-necked foes as mighty enemies which are vulnerable to His all-sufficient, all-prevailing might, are the sort of people who are going to enjoy the fullness of Christ. Are you a spiritual optimist, or a spiritual pessimist as you recognize the giant?

The Giant "Flesh" Is Gigantic in Influence

Christ said, "That which is born of the flesh is flesh" (John 3:6). Every human being born into this world receives physical life from physical parents, and also the principle of sin (the flesh) from parents who are indwelt by the self-same principle. In the same way that physical life begets physical life, the flesh reproduces itself in the human race from generation to generation. Thus, every human being is born of the flesh, both in the sense of the physical birth and sinful principle. "All have sinned," because all are sinners, and all are sinners because sin is resident within them from the day of their birth. The whole human race is under the gigantic influence of the giant "flesh."

The Giant "Flesh" Is Gigantic in Ability

The flesh can be recognized quite simply. Galatians 5:17 (Amplified New Testament) states, "For the desires of the flesh are opposed to the (Holy) Spirit, and the (desires of the) Spirit are opposed to the flesh (Godless human nature); for these are antagonistic to each other — continually withstanding and in conflict with each other — so that you are not free but are prevented from doing what you desire to do." Therefore the flesh is all that the Spirit of God is not, and is the complete antithesis to the Spirit. The Spirit is called "the Spirit of God," therefore the flesh can be recognized in action as anything which is ungodly or un-Godlike.

The Spirit of Truth is another of His titles, and it is obvious that in his antagonism the flesh is a specialist in all brands of untruthfulness. Blatant lies, misrepresentations, deceitfulness and exaggerations are his masterpieces. The Spirit of Grace is the antithesis of all that is ungracious, rude, uncouth, vulgar and obscene, and these are all characteristics of the flesh. Love flows from the indwelling Spirit of God, and the opposite of love is hatred in many varied forms — violent opposition, back-biting, selfishness, hardness, intolerance. Peace typifies the Spirit and the flesh produces strife, discord and division.

Recognize the giant; see his characteristics and understand how deep-rooted is his tyranny in the human heart. "Now the doings (practices) of the flesh are clear — obvious: they are immorality, impurity, indecency; Idolatry, sorcery, enmity, strife, jealousy, anger (ill temper), selfishness, divisions (dissensions), party spirit (factions, sects with peculiar opinions, heresies); Envy, drunkenness, carousing, and the like" (Galatians 5:19-21, Amplified New Testament).

THE GIANT "FLESH" IS GIGANTIC IN VERSATILITY

He is remarkably adaptable in all situations. He may show himself as a brash braggart until he suffers a major set-back through being exposed for what he is in front of friends. Immediately he will switch to slimy self-pity and will crawl with humility. When he functions as a brash braggart, he seeks to be the center of attention, and of course his self-pity and pseudo-sorrowful demeanor are designed to produce the identical result.

Religion is a favorite hobby of the giant "flesh." He turned out religion in Saul of Tarsus for years. "If any other man considers that he has or seems to have reason to rely on the flesh and his physical and outward advantages, still more have I! Circumcised when I was eight days old, of the race of Israel, of the tribe of Benjamin, a Hebrew (and the son) of Hebrews; as to the observance of the Law I was of (the party of) the Pharisees, As to my zeal I was a persecutor of the church, and by the Law's standard of righteousness — (supposed) justice, uprightness and right standing with God — I was proven to be blameless and no fault was found with me" (Philippians 3:4-6, Amplified New Testament). The giant "flesh" was delighted to dominate the life of Paul and showed himself gigantic in zeal, earnestness, effort, endeavor and religious observance.

Possibly one of the finest exposés of the giant "flesh" in Scripture is Job's sickly, fleshly "ode to myself" recorded in Job 29. "I washed my steps with butter" — *self-indulgence*. "When I went out . . . . The young men saw me . . . the princes refrained talking . . . the nobles held their peace" — *self-importance*. "When the ear heard me, then it blessed me" — *self-opinion*. "I delivered the poor . . . I caused the widow's heart to sing for joy" — *self-praise*. "I put on righteousness and it clothed me" — *self-righteousness*. This, of course, was Job's main difficulty — he was full of himself and a slave to that versatile giant, the "flesh."

The flesh has no objection to turning evangelical. Giant "flesh" is prepared to adapt himself to the Gospel, and in the young Church at Galatia he made an attempt to wreck the fellowship by taking over the lives of the newly-converted Christians, and he was almost successful. Paul intervened and wrote, "Are you so foolish and so senseless and so silly? Having begun (your new life spiritually) with the (Holy) Spirit, are you now reaching perfection (by dependence) on the flesh?" (Galatians 3:3, Amplified New Testament). The flesh will organize a church fellowship, preach a sermon, lead the singing, cross an ocean to the heathen, and generally make havoc wherever he may go.

He can be charitable, sociable, amiable, likable. Self-indulgence and self-abnegation are all part of his repertoire. He is a giant in activity, boundless in scope, amazing in adaptability. He is dangerous and deadly, so search him out and recognize him.

CALEB RECKONED WITH GOD

The difference between Caleb and Joshua and the other ten spies was that the former recognized the giants and reckoned with God, and the latter recognized the giants and did not reckon with God. Caleb and Joshua got a view of the giants from God's angle, and the others got a view of the giants from the grasshopper's angle.

Caleb's thinking was wonderfully clear: "Here we have big giants, a wonderful land and God's promises. God has promised us the land; the land is occupied by giants; therefore God has the answer to the giants. Obviously He intends us to know the answer, so we will reckon with Him and go ahead." When Caleb said, "We are well able to overcome it" (Numbers 13: 30), he was not being impulsive, idealistic or irresponsible, for he added later, "If the Lord delight in us, then he will bring us into this land, and give it us, a land which floweth with milk and honey. Only rebel not ye against the Lord, neither fear ye the people of the land; for they are bread for us: their defence is departed from them, and the Lord is with us: fear them not" (Numbers 14:8, 9).

Caleb was a hundred per cent realistic, with his feet planted firmly on the ground, but his heart anchored firmly in the heavenlies. Problems, difficulties, dangers, and hardships were common in his daily life, but his God was in control, and therefore the giants' days were numbered as far as he was concerned. In his eyes the giants were vulnerable and defeated because of the vivid reality of the Lord in his life. Therefore he commanded, "Fear them not." Retreat and defeat were unthinkable; advance was obvious; and victory assured, simply because, "The Lord is with us."

Let us be realistic about the giant "flesh." Has God promised the fullness of Christ? Of course He has. Is the giant "flesh" opposed to this? Naturally! Has God reckoned with the flesh, or did the giant take Him by surprise? Ridiculous! Then has God the answer to the flesh? Emphatically, yes! Then what is the answer?

God Has Condemned the Flesh

Sin entered when "freewill" became "I will." "I will" rebelled against God, and Satan fell. Satan seduced Eve — she agreed and said, "I will." Eve seduced Adam — Cain and Abel were born physically and inherited the old "I will" — sin, self and the flesh. The human race multiplied, and the flesh grew into gigantic proportions.

The origin of sin was a tragedy of the greatest magnitude. God was disobeyed and His authority repudiated. The history of sin has been one long chapter of misery, suffering and despair. The character of the flesh has not changed, and the rebellion and resistance to God is just as evident today as it ever was. What then would one expect God's attitude to the flesh to be? The origin, history, attitude and products of the flesh are totally anti-God and therefore it is obvious that God always has been and always will be unrelenting in His antagonism to the flesh. He condemns the flesh out of hand. The flesh in its many guises, religious or reprobate, cultured or cruel, intelligent or ignorant, is sin, and as such is utterly condemned by God. The giant has been tried, the sentence has been passed, and God's verdict is, "The flesh is condemned."

Paul says, "In my flesh dwelleth no good thing" (Romans 7:18). Argue and resist this dogmatic statement if you will, but the Truth of God stands firm — "no good thing." The giant becomes upset about this definition of himself and his ability, and loves to plead his own case. "But I do good things. I sing in the choir; I help other people; I give to charity," etc. Never be misled by this, but always measure goodness by God's standard, and not by man's standard. The outward activities of the flesh may look remarkably good, but the source is rotten. Sometimes fruit on a tree looks glorious, but owing to a disease of the tree, the fruit is rotten inside, and this is true as far as the flesh is concerned, for God says there is no good thing in it.

"They that are in the flesh cannot please God" (Romans 8:8). This is not surprising, for how can a system diametrically opposed to God be expected to please God? Naturally the last thing that the flesh has in mind is God's plan and purpose, and the last thing the flesh desires to do is to please God. Even if the flesh desired to please God, it could not, for it does not have the ability to reproduce the quality of living that alone brings pleasure to God.

Christ said, "The flesh profiteth nothing" (John 6: 63). The flesh in all its versatility, energy and activity does not and cannot please God, and in the eternal economy profits nothing. Giant "flesh" is a grasshopper in God's sight. Giant "flesh" is condemned. This is good news for disillusioned saints, but there is much more wonderful news to come.

GOD HAS CRUCIFIED THE FLESH

God has condemned the flesh, but also as far as God is concerned, the execution has already taken place. Giant flesh has a long neck, and God has administered the death blow with unerring accuracy. Listen to the good news: the giant before whom you fled has been condemned and crucified by God who will give you the land. Therefore, reckon with God as Caleb did, for God knows the giant better than you do, and his "defence is departed" from him. God says so, and God cannot lie!

The execution took place almost two thousand years ago outside Jerusalem. Jesus Christ, God's Son, died for sinners, and for sin. This is the essence of the glorious message of substitution. However, Scripture teaches that when Christ died, God looks upon all those "in Christ" (whether they lived before, after or contemporary with Christ is irrelevant to the God of eternity), as if they died in Him. The flesh has been crucified with Christ.

Paul grasped this, and said, "I have been crucified with Christ" (Galatians 2:20, Amplified New Testament). Teaching the Romans the fundamentals of the faith he asked, "Are you ignorant of the fact that all of us who have been baptized into Christ Jesus were baptized into His death? We were buried therefore with Him by the baptism into death, so that just as

Christ was raised from the dead by the glorious (power) of the Father, so we too might habitually live and behave in newness of life" (Romans 6:3, 4, Amplified New Testament), and "We know that our old (unrenewed) self was nailed to the cross with Him in order that (our) body, (which is the instrument) of sin, might be made ineffective and inactive for evil, that we might no longer be the slaves of sin" (Romans 6:6, Amplified New Testament).

Many Christians experience grave difficulty over this point. They say, "The flesh cannot have been crucified because it still works," or, "I do not feel as if the flesh has been crucified." Naturally this does pose difficulties, but remember that we must look at this from God's viewpoint. God says that you have been crucified whatever you may feel, think or understand! Perhaps you do not believe that you died in Christ, but you do believe that Christ died for you.

Why do you believe that Christ died for you? You answer, "Because the Bible says so." Yes — and the Bible says you died in Christ, too. There is no way out of this — if you believe Christ died for you because the Bible says so, then you have no alternative to believing that you died in Christ and for the selfsame reason — the Bible says so. You may say, "But I do not understand it." Do you understand what it really means that Christ died for you? It is as impossible to plumb the depths of Christ's substitutionary death for you as it is to rationalize the doctrine of your identification with Him in death.

The death of Christ is a glorious mystery, but the Truth of God is clear as crystal. Christ died for you, and you died in Him. You must not believe one without the other, for His death for you clears you of sin's guilt and your death in Him rids you of the tryanny of the giant "flesh." Did you ever thank the Lord Jesus for dying for you? Of course you did, and at that moment you entered into the good of His substitutionary death. Then why not thank Him that you died in Him, and begin to enter into all that your death in Him secures for you? Thus you will not only recognize the giant, but reckon with God.

CALEB RECLAIMED THE GARRISON

After Caleb had spoken his mind about the land and the giants, God promised that he and Joshua would enter the land. Through Moses the Lord also said to His faithful servant, "Surely the land whereon thy feet have trodden shall be thine inheritance, and thy children's for ever, because thou hast wholly followed the Lord my God" (Joshua 14:9). The land whereon Caleb's feet had trodden was Hebron, and this city was a great and fenced garrison of giants. However, it had not always been so, for formerly Hebron had been Abraham's dwelling place. God had met with him there. Jacob and his sons lived in the area, and Hebron was the treasured last resting place of Abraham, Isaac, Jacob, Sarah, Rebekah, and Leah. Hebron means fellowship, and it was this beautiful place of fellowship which the giants had made into a garrison of evil. Caleb wanted to reclaim it, and possess it, and God gave it to him.

God is a giving God — "Thanks be to God which *giveth* us the victory" (I Corinthians 15:57). ". . . the living God who *giveth* us richly all things to enjoy" (I Timothy 6:17). God does the giving, but man must do the taking. Sometimes this is not fully understood. God gives you air, but He does not breathe it for you. He expects you to take what He gives. He gives you food and clothing, but He does not feed you and dress you. He leaves that to you. He gives eternal life, but you must accept the life He offers. Victory is His gift, but you must claim the victory and make it your own.

Caleb knew all this, and he had to wait forty-five years before he had an opportunity to take what God had promised. "And now, behold, the Lord hath kept me alive, as he said, these forty and five years, even since the Lord spake this word unto Moses, while the children of Israel wandered in the wilderness: and now, lo, I am this day fourscore and five years old. As yet I am as strong this day as I was in the day that Moses sent me: as my strength was then, even so is my strength now, for war, both to go out, and to come in. Now therefore give me this mountain, whereof the Lord spake in that day; for thou heardest in that day how the Anakims were there, and that the cities were great and fenced; if so be the Lord will be with me, then I shall be able to drive them out, as the Lord said" (Joshua 14:10-12). The result of his claim based on a forty-five-year-old promise was, "Hebron therefore became the inheritance of Caleb the son of Jephunneh the Kenezite unto this day, because that he wholly followed the Lord God of Israel" (Joshua 14:14). The garrison town indwelt by long-necked, vulnerable, already-defeated giants became his by right, because God gave it to him.

Let us pause here for a moment. Having read of God's finished work on Calvary and the blessings His finished work secured for you, have you ever realized that it is your right and privilege to claim the victory which God has promised to you and procured for you? If so, do not stop there, but do what Caleb did. With his title deeds in his pocket, and his sword in his hand, he marched on Hebron. He went into battle knowing full well that the victory was his, but that there would be no victory without a battle. The word, "victory," pre-supposes a battle, and all God's promises of victory automatically pre-suppose battles. Often Christians think that victory is possible without battle, but this is ludicrous. Every battle is a God-given opportunity to enjoy the victory which He gives.

The ensuing battle resulted in a victory which was a foregone conclusion, because Caleb went into battle rejoicing in the God who gives the victory. "And Caleb drove thence the three sons of Anak, Sheshai, and Ahiman, and Talmai, the children of Anak" (Joshua 15:14). This victory was even more wonderful because the rest of the Israelites were not so successful, for when they tried to conquer their opponents, "they were not able to drive them out." It only remains now for us to discover how to take the victory that God gives. How does one enjoy the victory that God gives over the giant "flesh"?

1. *Believe the Truth*

God says the flesh is carnal, condemned and crucified. Decide if you believe this.

2. *Claim the Promise*

God has promised victory over the giant because of what He has already done. In the same way that He promised you eternal life as a gift and you asked for it and thanked Him on receipt, so now ask Him for His victory *and thank Him for it.*

3. *Go Into Battle*

With the title deeds of God's Word in your heart, "Sin shall not have dominion over you" (Romans 6: 14), and "Knowing this, that our old man is crucified with him, that the body of sin might be destroyed, that henceforth we should not serve sin. For he that is

dead is freed from sin" (Romans 6:6, 7). Engage the
enemy in combat knowing that the victory is yours.
When the defeated giant, "flesh," raises his ugly head
and the battle is on, obey God's Word.

a. ". . . reckon yourselves also to be dead indeed
unto sin, but alive unto God through Jesus Christ our
Lord." With a cool, calm, collected assurance, look
the giant "flesh" straight in the eye, and reckon yourself to be unresponsive to him and no longer under
any obligation to fear him or serve him.

b. "Let not therefore sin reign in your mortal
body, that you should obey it in the lusts thereof"
(Romans 6:12). With a definite act of your will, refuse
the defeated giant the right to take possession of your
mortal body.

c. ". . . Neither yield ye your members as instruments of unrighteousness unto sin" (Romans 6:13).
When the uncouth giant grabs one of your members,
repudiate his right, and forbid him to use your members to his own degraded ends.

d. ". . . but yield yourselves unto God, as those
that are alive from the dead, and your members as
instruments of righteousness unto God" (Romans 6:
13). Positively, at the moment of battle, present the
member which the flesh wishes to use and abuse, to
the One who lives in the power of His resurrection
within you, that He might use that member for His
own glory. This is what you must do. This is how
you take what God gives.

Also remember, ". . . they that are Christ's have
crucified the flesh with the affections and lusts" (Galatians 5:24). There is no contradiction here with what
has already been said. God has crucified the flesh, and
they that are Christ's fully agree with this drastic execution, and cooperate with God in keeping the giant

where he belongs — in his tomb. This means that "they that are Christ's" gladly, willingly and intelligently say "no" to the insinuations of the giant they used to fear, and before whom they used to flee.

Constantly bear in mind Philippians 3:3 which says that true Christians have "no confidence in the flesh." This means that you must constantly reject the flesh and recognize the flesh's deceitfulness and degradation, and place your utter confidence in your Risen Victor.

The results of these actions are a foregone conclusion on the basis of God's finished work, and unfailing promises. The victory is yours!

It is lovely to see what happened in Hebron as a result of Caleb's victory. In the early days, Hebron was the place of fellowship, but as we have already seen, it became the home of a giant. Then the Lord gave it to Caleb as his possession, and Caleb took what God gave and "expelled thence the three sons of Anak" (Judges 1:20). Then Hebron was chosen to be a "city of refuge" (Joshua 20:7), and in later days the town became the "seat of a King" (II Samuel 2:11).

You cannot afford to miss the victory, because your life is created to be the place of fellowship, and not the home of the giant "flesh." The fullness of Christ is yours through claiming and taking, in order that your life might become a city of refuge and the seat of a King.

9

Full of Good Works

DORCAS PASSED AWAY, BUT HER TESTIMONY LIVED ON. ". . . this woman was full of good works" (Acts 9:36). Peter was called to Joppa, and the Lord used him to raise Dorcas from the dead, so there was no need to erect a tombstone for the deceased. If a tombstone had been erected I feel sure that the following sentiments would have been engraved upon it: "Here lies Dorcas — a woman who in her lifetime was full of good works." The disciples mourned her, for they loved her and honored her. Many of them had been ministered to by her, for she was essentially a practical believer. The Christianity of Dorcas worked out through her finger tips and found expression in all manner of works.

We have been discussing a glorious truth — the fullness of Christ — and it may seem strange that we have now deserted such thrilling themes as "fullness," "fruitfulness," "victory," "all-sufficiency," etc., to think about "the coats and garments which Dorcas made" (Acts 9:39). However, there is nothing strange about this at all, for the fullness of Christ invariably produces a life "full of good works." There is no such thing as a mature Christian experience which is not evidenced by sheer good works. The sparkling, snow-clad peaks of the Alps must slope down to the farms and the fields of the valleys. The lofty themes of spirituality must find expression in the lowly tasks of practicality if they

130

are to mean anything at all. The charge has often been leveled by non-Christians at professing Christians that they are "so heavenly-minded that they are no earthly good." This is totally contrary to all that God has in mind.

In some ecclesiastical circles a "social gospel" is preached. Basically, this gospel is a gospel of works. "Be good and kind and helpful, love your neighbor as yourself, and God will do the decent thing and be good and kind and helpful to you, and He will love you for all that you have done." This is not the Gospel that Paul preached, for this gospel requires no cross, no resurrection, no atonement, no judgment, and no Holy Spirit. "But even if we or an angel from heaven should preach to you a gospel contrary to and different from that which we preached to you, let him be accursed — anathema, devoted to destruction, doomed to eternal punishment! As we said before, so I now say again, If anyone is preaching to you a gospel different from or contrary to that which you received (from us), let him be accursed — anathema, devoted to destruction, doomed to eternal punishment!" (Galatians 1:8, 9, Amplified New Testament). This "social gospel" must be avoided and shunned on the authority of God's Word, and this the evangelicals have done. Unfortunately, in some cases the "social gospel" has been shunned with such enthusiasm that the saints today have gone to the other extreme. The attitude expressed is: "We must be very careful to avoid the subject of works, or people may get hold of the idea that they can be saved by works." It is tremendously important that we get this subject of works in perspective.

WORKS IN PERSPECTIVE

Ephesians 2:8, 9 is very clear: "For by grace are ye saved through faith; and that not of yourselves: it is the gift of God: Not of works, lest any man should boast." "Not of works" is emphasized, and quite rightly so. Unfortunately however, the fact that Ephesians 2:10 follows hard on the heels of Ephesians 2:9 is often completely overlooked. "For we are . . . created in Christ Jesus unto good works." "Not of works" and "unto good works" must be stressed equally. Many godly people today are guilty of error, for they have failed to understand the significance of their salvation. They were saved "unto good works which God hath before ordained." The message of salvation outlined in these three verses is:

1. Saved
2. *By* grace
3. *Through* faith
4. *Unto* works

and it is impossible to take away any one of these basic factors. No informed Christian would ever suggest that salvation is by grace without faith, or by faith without grace; and no informed Christian must ever be found guilty of suggesting either by his life or his ministry that salvation is not "unto good works."

It is glorious that man can appropriate the unlimited grace of God through faith. How wonderful then to know that the saved sinner, at the moment of his salvation, was slotted into God's fore-ordained pattern to be an instrument of good works which have already been planned to form an integral part of God's divine plan. This is the wonderful news of the Gospel.

Evidently James, the Lord's brother, had encountered a similar tendency to the one outlined above, in the Early Church, for he wrote: "What is the use (profit), my brethren, for any one to profess to have faith if he has no (good) works (to show for it)? Can (such) faith save (his soul)?" (James 2:14, Amplified New Testament), and then he stated, "So also faith if it does not have works (deeds and actions of obedience to back it up), by itself is destitute of power — inoperative, dead" (James 2:17, Amplified New Testament), and in blunt language he added, "Are you willing to be shown (proof), you foolish, unproductive, spiritually-deficient fellow, that faith apart from (good) works is inactive and ineffective and worthless?" (James 2:20, Amplified New Testament).

The whole point of his argument was that if faith does not work, it is not real faith. The proof of faith is not in words, but in works. He used Abraham as an example. "Was not our forefather Abraham (shown to be) justified — made acceptable to God — by (his) works when he brought to the altar as an offering his (own) son Isaac?" (James 2:21, Amplified New Testament). The glorious faith of Abraham is spoken of throughout the world, but always remember that it was demonstrated in his life by what he did. One day, in sheer naked obedience and faith, he tied his only son to an altar and was ready to kill him at God's command, knowing full well that God would raise him up. It was his work of faith that demonstrated his depth of faith.

"So also with Rahab the harlot" (James 2:25, Amplified New Testament). She believed God and was prepared to confess Him with her mouth: ". . . for the Lord your God, he is God in heaven above, and in earth beneath" (Joshua 2:11), but the reality of her faith was not demonstrated by what she said, but by what she did. She took a calculated risk when she sheltered the spies in her home, but this was the tangible evidence of her faith in the Living God. She was prepared to witness to her faith by works which entailed inconvenience, danger and certain death if she was discovered.

Paul left Titus in Crete to "set right what was defective, and finish what was left undone" (Titus 1:5, Amplified New Testament). His ministry was to lead people to Christ and then lead them on to maturity — "the measure of the stature of the fullness of Christ." Paul wrote to him to remind him of the responsibilities of this ministry, and said,

> But when the goodness and loving kindness of God our Savior to man (as man) appeared, He saved us, not because of any works of righteousness that we had done, but because of His own pity and mercy, by (the) cleansing (bath) of the new birth (regeneration) and renewing of the Holy Spirit, Which He poured out (so) richly upon us through Jesus Christ our Savior. (And He did it in order) that we might be justified by His grace — by His favor, wholly undeserved, that is, that we might be acknowledged and counted as conformed to the Divine will in purpose, thought and action; and that we might become heirs of eternal life according to (our) hope. This message is most trustworthy, and concerning these things I want you to insist steadfastly, so that those who have believed in (trusted, relied on) God may be careful to apply themselves to honorable occupations and to doing good, for such things are (not only) excellent and right (in themselves), but (they are) good and profitable for the people (Titus 3:4-8, Amplified New Testament).

He asked Titus to "*insist steadfastly*" that man is not saved by any "works of righteousness" which he has done, but by grace through faith, *but* that having been saved, he must be careful to apply himself to "honourable occupations and to doing good" — *not of works but unto good works!* When we get "works in perspective" we will understand the importance of works in the life of a mature Christian. Works are important because:

(1) As we have already seen, God saves people and leaves them on earth to do a job of work which He has planned for them in advance.

(2) Jesus said, "Let your light so shine before men, that they may see your good works, and glorify your Father which is in heaven" (Matthew 5:16). The world must be reached with the Gospel, and it must be made to realize that the Gospel is "the power of God." *Shouting* will not always make this clear, but *shining* will! Therefore, the Master commanded that the faith of His disciples should be gloriously evident in recognizable, tangible works. This is a lesson that needs to be preached and declared with utmost clarity in the twentieth century. The man in the street is not usually impressed by doctrinal arguments or theological niceties, but he is most impressed by a life that demonstrates in practical good works a quality of experience which is foreign to his own. Often when a man sees this kind of living, he is convicted of his own sinfulness, and brought to the point of inquiry and discovery of Christ for himself.

(3) The Judgment Seat of Christ awaits every believer: "For we must all appear and be revealed as we are before the judgment seat of Christ, so that each one may receive (his pay) according to what he has done in the body, whether good or evil, (considering what his purpose and motive have been, and what he has achieved, been busy with and given himself and his attention to accomplishing)" (II Corinthians 5:10, Amplified New Testament); "For no other foundation can any one lay than that which is (already) laid, which is Jesus Christ, the Messiah, the Anointed One. But if anyone builds upon the Foundation, whether it be with gold, silver, precious stones, wood, hay, straw, The work of each (one) will become (plainly, openly)

known — shown for what it is; for the day (of Christ) will disclose and declare it, because it will be revealed with fire, and the fire will test and critically appraise the character and worth of the work each person has done. If the work which any person has built on this Foundation — any product of his efforts whatever — survives (this test), he will get his reward. But if any person's work is burned up (under the test), he will suffer the loss (of it all, losing his reward), though he himself will be saved, but only as (one who has passed) through fire" (I Corinthians 3:11-15, Amplified New Testament). God in His loving kindness reveals some aspects of eternity to His children in advance, and one of the most important of these pre-revealed eternal events is the Judgment Seat of Christ. Every believer will stand before the Lord (not to be judged for his sin, for he has been forgiven and justified), but in order that his works might be examined. The Lord will determine the rewards of His servants on the basis of works done subsequent to conversion. This is a sobering thought!

It is the quality of work that He will evaluate, ". . . because it will be revealed with fire, and the fire will test and critically appraise the character and worth of the work each person has done" (I Corinthians 3:13, Amplified New Testament). The test will "critically appraise the character and worth of the work."

This demonstrates the grace and justice of God, for some of His children are more gifted than others, and therefore capable of greater productivity. For instance, Paul, with his massive intellect and first-class education was better equipped for his outstanding work than the humble Dorcas. However, Paul's preaching and Dorcas' needle-work will both be evaluated by their quality, and not by their quantity.

On the great day many impressive edifices will be shown to consist of nothing more than wood, hay and stubble, and at the same time the gold, silver and precious stones of faithful service stemming from a heart experience of the fullness of Christ will be revealed and rewarded for all eternity.

"If I (can) speak in the tongues of men and (even) of angels, but have not love (that reasoning, intentional, spiritual devotion such as is inspired by God's love for and in us), I am only a noisy gong or a clanging cymbal. And if I have prophetic powers — that is, the gift of interpreting the divine will and purpose; and understand all the secret truths and mysteries and possess all knowledge, and if I have (sufficient) faith so that I can remove mountains, but have not love (God's love in me) I am nothing — a useless nobody. Even if I dole out all that I have (to the poor in providing) food, and if I surrender my body to be burned (or in order that I may glory), but have not love (God's love in me), I gain nothing" (I Corinthians 13:1-3, Amplified New Testament). The "character and worth" of all work is determined by the motive power behind the work. If God's love filling and flooding your heart is not the sole motive of your Christian service and good works, then you are busy producing fuel for a bonfire, regardless of how impressed your church or missionary society may be with you.

WORKS IN PRINCIPLE

"Therefore, my dear ones, as you have always obeyed (my suggestions), so now, not only (with the enthusiasm you would show) in my presence but much more because I am absent, work out — cultivate, carry out to the goal and fully complete — your own salvation with reverence and awe and trembling (self-distrust, that is, with serious caution, tenderness of conscience, watchfulness against temptation; timidly shrinking from whatever might offend God and discredit the name of Christ). (Not in your own strength) for it is God Who is all the while effectually at work in you — energizing and creating in you the power and desire — both to will and to work for His good pleasure and satisfaction and delight" (Philippians 2:12, 13, Amplified New Testament).

God at work in a man is the sole source of effective activity. Remember "the reality of who He is" . . . *He is God*. Think of the "reality of where He is" . . . it is God *in you*. Consider the "reality of why He is who He is where He is" . . . God is at work in you "both to will and to work for His good pleasure and satisfaction and delight." He saved you unto foreordained good works and is ready to work in you, that which is well-pleasing to Himself: in other words, His own foreordained plan. Works produced on any other principle are worthless and useless, for the Psalmist said, "Except the Lord build the house, they labor in vain that build it" (Psalm 127:1).

Paul said, "For He Who motivated and fitted Peter and worked effectively through him for the mission to the circumcised, motivated and fitted me and worked through me also for (the mission to) the Gentiles" (Galatians 2:8, Amplified New Testament). Paul and Peter were as different as chalk and cheese, but they both had within them the dynamic of the Living God, and they both demonstrated through their lives the effectiveness of His divine activity in good works. It was as pointless for Peter to want to be Paul because he envied Paul's intelligence as it was for Paul to wish he were Peter in order that he could be the apostle to his beloved Jews. They both realized that they had been fitted and equipped by God for a particular task, and also that God Himself was mightily at work in them and through them, accomplishing His own task.

Do not long *to be someone else,* because He made you ideal for His plan. Do not continually seek *to do something else,* because He knows what He is doing. All you have to do is to make sure that He is working effectively through you. If He is, then the world will see Him in your works. The plan of God will be fulfilled through you, and eternity will reveal the gold, silver and precious stones of your good works.

Works In Practice

The Church at Thessalonica was one of the greatest spiritual wonders of all time. Paul held a series of meetings in the heathen city lasting between three and four weeks (Acts 17:2), and in that period many people stepped out of black heathendom into the knowledge of the Lord Jesus Christ, and a small church was founded. This church in a remarkably short time became "a pattern to all the believers" (I Thessalonians 1:7, Amplified New Testament). When God is at work He can build an ideal church in the midst of black heathendom in the space of three or four weeks, provided the individual members mean business.

The members of this ideal church had works in perspective, for we read that they "turned to God from idols to *serve* the Living and true God; And to wait for his Son from heaven, . . . " (I Thessalonians 1: 9, 10). First they were saved, then they served, and all the time they anticipated the Second Coming of the Lord Jesus.

It is important to notice that their service was directed toward the *"living* and *true God."* Work done in the name of the *Living* God must be characterized by *vitality*. The Living God is not interested in dead, dry works. The world remains coldly unimpressed by purely mechanical works and enemy territory can only be invaded when service is dynamically vital. The True God is quick to discern the *validity* of all works, for He knows all hypocrisy and rejects it completely. Therefore, all works must be characterized by vitality and validity, and it takes the dynamic of God Himself to produce works of such vitality and the love of God alone can motivate works of intrinsic validity.

"Whatsoever ye do, do it heartily, as to the Lord and not unto men; Knowing that of the Lord ye shall receive the reward of the inheritance: for ye serve the Lord Christ" (Colossians 3:23, 24). "Ye serve the Lord Christ" and your works are intended to represent all that He is, because they are the outworking of all that He is in you. Colossians 3 gives many clues to the areas in which the fullness of Christ is intended to be expressed in the fullness of works:

In the World

"Mortify therefore your members which are *upon the earth*" (v. 5). In the midst of all that typifies the world — uncleanness, covetousness (v. 5), anger, wrath, malice and filth (v. 8), your works are to stand out like a beacon. Instead of uncleanness, your works will be pure. Covetousness will be abandoned for "givingness." Anger and wrath will not be seen, but instead grace and love will demonstrate the fullness of Christ even in the face of bitter opposition and scathing ridicule. It is your works that will shine in the world. The world would sit up and take notice if every Christian knew what it was to live a life of good works!

In the Church

"As the elect of God, holy and beloved . . ." (v. 12). The true Church is composed of "God's own picked representatives" (v. 12, Amplified New Testament) who, having been purified and made holy by God, experience the love of God. In this community works of sheer goodness are to be expected. Nehemiah expected works from the small church that he organized in the rebuilding of the walls of Jerusalem, but he was disappointed with some members for "the nobles put not their necks to the work of their Lord" (Nehemiah 3:5). The church is intended to buzz with divine activity as each redeemed member goes about his Father's business. Does your church fit this description, or do you have too many nobles with necks that will not bend?

In the Home

"Wives" (v. 18), "husbands" (v. 19), "children" (v. 20), "fathers" (v. 21). It is a proven fact that most juvenile delinquency stems from broken homes or inadequate home life. Divorces and separation are a disgrace to many "civilized" nations. It is because of the total lack of the presence of Christ in all His fullness in such homes that these tragedies occur. However, it is possible for a Christian home to be occupied by wives, husbands, children, etc., who fail to manifest the fullness of Christ in their works of goodness, kindness, tolerance, patience, helpfulness and love, and the result is discord and strife and a parody of a Christian home. Works demonstrate faith, glorify God, and adorn and enrich a home when the Lord is at work in it. "And it was noised that He was in the house" (Mark 2:1) could, and should, be, a true description of every home inhabited by a Christian.

In the Place of Work

"Servants" (v. 22), "masters" (Colossians 4:1). Whether you employ or are employed is irrelevant to the Master. He is concerned that if you are an employee, your work should glorify Him, and that if you are an employer, your fairness, integrity and honesty should demonstrate all that He is in you. Many souls have been attracted to Christ as they have seen Him consistently and conscientiously at work in a humble laborer or in a prosperous executive of a corporation; on the other hand inconsistency in the works of professing believers has been a stumbling block to innumerable souls.

If you have "works" in perspective and you recognize that the Lord Himself is ready to work wherever you are at any given moment, may I suggest that you now lay aside this book, take a pencil and paper and make a list of people whom you think God wishes to reach through "good works." Then make a list of your talents and think how God could conceivably use them for His glory. Finally, make a list of your possessions — home, car, bank balance, leisure time, and decide how He could use your home to meet with seeking souls. Discover if He could operate through your car as you share it with others. Perhaps your bank balance should be put to divine work. Do you spend your leisure time or do you invest it? Would it not be a good idea to help some older person, visit a hospital, or take a child from an orphanage to the beach? The Lord Jesus works in this way in these days! God's message to disgruntled saints through Isaiah was: "Is not this the fast that I have chosen? to loose the bands of wickedness, to undo the heavy burdens, and to let the oppressed go free, and that ye break every yoke? Is it not to deal thy bread to the hungry, and that thou bring the poor that are cast out to thy house? when thou seest the naked, that thou cover him; and that thou hide not thyself from thine own flesh? Then shall thy light break forth as the morning, and thine health shall spring forth speedily: and thy righteousness shall go before thee; the glory of the Lord shall be thy re-reward" (Isaiah 58:6-8).

10

A Net Full of Fish

IT WAS A GREAT DAY FOR GENNESARET WHEN THE MASTER came to preach. He made a boat His pulpit and the shore His auditorium. The sand and pebbles became pews, and the vast congregation listened to His message with rapt attention. There was such interest and enthusiasm that "the people pressed upon him to hear the word of God" (Luke 5:1).

At the conclusion of His talk, the Master turned to practical application. He said, "Launch out into the deep and let down your nets for a draught" (Luke 5:4). Peter enjoyed the ministry immensely, but he was decidedly apprehensive about the practical application. "Master, we have toiled all the night, and have taken nothing" — but with a suspicion of reluctance he added — "Nevertheless at thy word I will let down the net" (Luke 5:5). Many Christians become extremely excited about conventions and meetings, preachers and books, but they show scant enthusiasm for practical commands like "launch out" and "let down." "Listening in" is wonderful (there is no cost involved), but "launching out" is not so good. "Looking up" is delightful, but "letting down" poses special problems.

The Lord said to His early disciples, "Follow me, and I will make you fishers of men" (Matthew 4:19). The responsibility of the disciples was to follow, and the Master's responsibility was to make them fishers

144

of men. Are you a fisher of men? Have you launched
out and let down, or is your boat firmly anchored to a
church pew?

The answer to these questions is vitally important.
Jesus said, "I *will* make you fishers of men *if* you follow
me." Therefore, if you are not a fisher of men, either
you are not following, or His promise is not true. Obviously, you know that the second alternative is unthinkable, and therefore the incontrovertible fact is
that if there is no fishing, there is no following. Caleb
proved that "following" means "fullness," and therefore
"no fishing" means "no following," and "no following"
means "no fullness." A man living in the fullness of
Christ is automatically a fisher of men.

When the Master called men "fish," He used a
term full of meaning. Men are darting hither and
thither in the shallows of aimlessness, busy doing nothing, and getting nowhere. They swim in shoals because
they lack the moral caliber to think, decide and act
independently on the basis of what they know to be
right. Consequently, they are jumping for the tiniest,
gaudiest flies in an effort to satisfy their hunger, only
to return to the depths of despair, emptiness and fu-
tility. Countless fish are drifting and floating with the
tides of moral laxity and spiritual bankruptcy today,
and the Master says, "Launch out" and "let down."

The church is the harbor, but the world outside
is the fishing ground, and "launch out" means "go
where the fish are." The boat that never goes fishing
will never make a profit for the master, and the redeemed soul who never launches out is bankrupt in the
extreme. "Launch out," even if it is uncomfortably
damp at times. It is worth it. "Let down your nets,"
knowing full well that it will mean that effort must
be expended, meal times may be suspended, the work-

ing day extended, and much leisure time ended — but it is the Christian's duty and should be his delight.

We would not expect a church with one hundred members to make much impact on a city of one and a half million inhabitants. In the first century it would have been different, for no doubt a church of this size would have made its presence felt, and the city would have known about it. Unfortunately, in the twentieth century things tend to be rather different. Why is this? The Early Church had fishers of men who "launched out" and "let down," but the present-day church has far too many members who sit tight.

The hypothetical church of one hundred members could do wonderful things if every member was a fisher of men. If one hundred members of one church caught one fish each year for fifteen years, the one and a half million population of the city would be in Christ's net, plus one hundred thousand visitors who happened to be in the city during that period. This is a staggering thought, and yet it is a question of simple mathematics. I do not know of any fisherman who would be satisfied with one fish per year, but I do know that the Master would be delighted in these days if each fisher of men could manage to catch one fish per year.

Fishermen never fish in swimming pools, for they know perfectly well that they would never catch fish there. Even God cannot save souls in church services which are attended exclusively by redeemed sinners, and yet how often churches pray that God will "send them in and save them," when all the time God has commanded, "go out and catch them." Fishermen know that fish do not give themselves up, but they have to be caught. The Lord Jesus was always looking for fish, and His disciples must do the same, for men do not surrender in these days — they have to be won to

Christ. Fishermen are dedicated to their task, but one gets the impression that many churches today are more dedicated to raising funds than catching fish. Fishermen expect to catch fish, but how many Christians anticipate leading others to Christ, and how many churches are equipped to deal with a large catch? The Church of Jesus Christ desperately needs fishermen, and remember that effective fishing is an inevitable consequence of the fullness of Christ.

FISHING TYPES

Small boys, old men, business magnates and office clerks, brown-skinned Polynesians and fur-wrapped Eskimos, all go fishing. Some have a butterfly net and a jam-jar; others have launches and equipment costing vast amounts of money, but they all enjoy fishing. There is no special type of person who makes a fisherman, the sole requirement being an interest in fish.

The Bible speaks about special gifts, but remains silent on the gifts of fishermen, because there is no special gift required or provided. Every Christian — a fisher of men — is Christ's ideal. I believe emphatically that every Christian should be effective as a soul-winner, and moreover *will* be effective as and when he lives in the joyful experience of Christ's fullness.

Do I hear murmurs of protest? Christ promised to *make* fishermen, and if He is responsible for the making, then it is impossible to doubt His ability to make even the most unpromising and unlikely Christian into an effective fisherman.

"I am not eloquent . . . I am slow of speech and of a slow tongue" (Exodus 4:10), cried Moses when commissioned as a fisher of men. He produced remarkably eloquent excuses for a man bereft of eloquence, and his rapid answer to God's command was most commendable for a man of a slow tongue! Moses simply used an excuse that has been used a thousand times since that day. If you can talk about the weather, you can talk about Christ, and talking about Christ in the energy of the Spirit is the stuff of effective witnessing.

"I am a man of unclean lips . . ." (Isaiah 6:5), said the prophet, but the Lord dealt with that problem, and Isaiah cried, "Here am I; send me." If, like Isaiah, you feel that you are not worthy to fish for men, you are quite right — you are not worthy, and you never will be. But if God tells you to fish, and equips you to do the job, then your unworthiness is His concern, and continual expressions of unworthiness are nothing more than excuses.

"Ah, Lord God! behold, I cannot speak: for I am a child" (Jeremiah 1:6), cried the mournful prophet. This was a fine statement from a man who could not speak! He proved himself wrong by the very statement that he made! If you have a tongue in your mouth, a brain in your head, and Christ in your heart, you can speak, and God says, "Say not, I am a child: for thou shalt go to all that I shall send thee, and whatsoever I command thee thou shalt speak" (Jeremiah 1:7).

Naaman's little maid landed a big fish when she caught the general (II Kings 5:2). And she was just a little slave girl, miles from home, living in an alien land.

The woman of Samaria caught a netful of fish when ". . . many of the Samaritans of that city believed on him . . ." (John 4:39), and she had not been to theological college or even attended a course on personal evangelism. In fact, she was only converted a few minutes before she started fishing.

The maniac of Gadara was told to go fishing as soon as he was liberated from the devil's dominion. "Go home to thy friends, and tell them how great things the Lord hath done for thee, and hath had compassion on thee" (Mark 5:19). He was feared and despised, an outcast from society, but he fished in the power of His Saviour.

Who can be an effective fisherman? *Anyone* and *everyone* with a tongue in their mouth, a brain in their head, and Christ in their heart.

FISHING TACTICS

The basic tactic of fishing is to arrange circumstances so that fish and fisherman are in the same place at the same time. This can be difficult if the ocean is big and the boat is small, but modern fishing boats have fine equipment to put them in touch with the fish.

The Master is more interested in seeking souls than Christians will ever be. He knows where the fish are. Moreover, He will take the fisherman and put him in the right place at the right time. The only requirement is that the fisherman must be tuned into the Lord, and easily maneuverable — following fully in the fullness of Christ. When this is the case, the fisherman and the fish have a habit of getting together. When Christ lives and rules in you, He will bring you in contact with the soul seeking Him, and it will be your joy and privilege to catch him.

God saw Cornelius seeking, so he contacted Peter and put them together, and Peter caught a big fish. The heart desires of the Ethiopian eunuch were open secrets to Almighty God, so He put Philip in the middle of the desert just as the Ethiopian's chariot came along, and another fish was caught. Ananias was one of the bravest men of all time, for the Lord told him to go and meet Saul of Tarsus, and he went, knowing full well that Saul was coming to Damascus to arrest the Christians. Ananias landed a whale of a fish that day!

All the Master needs is an available life, and He will organize the details, and a full net will result. The fullness of Christ means a netful of fishes.

FISHING TECHNIQUES

Fish must be found. You will only find a fish in his natural habitat. Therefore, you must not be surprised if the unregenerate fish is more inclined to visit a pub than a church. He will have a home, profession, hobbies and problems, and in all of these areas of his life you will have opportunities to contact him. Do not expect to meet him on your own territory, but rather make the effort (and this can be costly) to go to his territory if necessary. Peter found that his fish lived in a Gentile home, but even though he found it distasteful, he went to the home, and Cornelius and his household were gloriously converted. It was most inconvenient for Philip to have to leave Samaria and travel to the desert, but he did so, and was rewarded. Ananias exposed himself to real danger when he walked into the lion's den, but he never regretted his action.

Christians must firmly grasp the fact that the vast majority of people will not be found in church nowadays, and therefore if they are to be found, it must be outside the church. It is unrealistic to assume that when notices of services are posted, and advertisements made, that the fish will swim into the harbor in shoals. The simple fact is that they will not, and they must be contacted where they are.

The net must be placed. When the Lord brings you into contact with a fish, you must then be able to explain plainly and simply how Jesus Christ is relevant to his life. Your life must be a glowing example of the truths that you are explaining. There is no short-cut to knowing the truth, and it is imperative that you know your facts, and love your Bible. Your language must be intelligible to your contact, and your love for him must be obvious. Sincerity, and love shining from you, the power of the Spirit upon you, and the Living Word presented by you, are all meshes in the net.

Placing the net may be a long, tedious process, but always remember that you have inexhaustible supplies of grace and patience in Christ in you, and constantly bear in mind how long Christ sought you.

The catch must be landed. Fishermen do not influence fish — they catch them! You must be able not only to explain the Gospel to the fish, but you must be able to land him — to lead him to Christ. Pray with him when he is ready, in the same way that you prayed to invite Christ to come into your life. Bring him to the point of assurance and thankfulness for all that he has in Christ. Look after him, care for him, lead him on, and teach him how to win others for Christ as soon as possible.

When Peter saw the tangible results of the Lord's working, he "fell down at Jesus' knees, saying, Depart from me; for I am a sinful man, O Lord, For he was astonished, and all that were with him, at the draught of the fishes which they had taken" (Luke 5:8, 9).

Conviction for his earlier faithlessness, amazement at the Lord's glorious ability and loving abandonment resulted from this episode, for once again the Lord showed that when He is given an opportunity, He works in unpredictable, but always superlative fashion. The fullness of Christ means a net full of fishes. Therefore, "launch out"; "let down"; and, by the way, you had better "look out"!